spirituality is for every body

spirituality is for every body

8 Accessible, Inclusive Ways to Connect with the Divine When Living with Disability

Allison V. Thompkins, Ph.D.

HAY HOUSE
Carlsbad, California • New York City
London • Sydney • New Delhi

Published in the United Kingdom by:
Hay House UK Ltd, The Sixth Floor, Watson House,
54 Baker Street, London W1U 7BU
Tel: +44 (0)20 3927 7290; Fax: +44 (0)20 3927 7291; www.hayhouse.co.uk

Published in the United States of America by:
Hay House Inc., PO Box 5100, Carlsbad, CA 92018-5100
Tel: (1) 760 431 7695 or (800) 654 5126
Fax: (1) 760 431 6948 or (800) 650 5115; www.hayhouse.com

Published in Australia by:
Hay House Australia Ltd, 18/36 Ralph St, Alexandria NSW 2015
Tel: (61) 2 9669 4299; Fax: (61) 2 9669 4144; www.hayhouse.com.au

Published in India by:
Hay House Publishers India, Muskaan Complex, Plot No.3, B-2,
Vasant Kunj, New Delhi 110 070
Tel: (91) 11 4176 1620; Fax: (91) 11 4176 1630; www.hayhouse.co.in

Cover design: Julie Davison
Interior design: Nick C. Welch
Author photo: Melissa Ortendahl Photography

A catalogue record for this book is available from the British Library.

Tradepaper ISBN: 978-1-83782-063-4
E-book ISBN: 978-1-4019-7493-0
Audiobook ISBN: 978-1-4019-7494-7

This product uses papers sourced from responsibly managed forests.
For more information, see www.hayhouse.co.uk.

Printed and bound by CPI Group (UK) Ltd, Croydon, CR0 4YY

dedication

I dedicate this book to my parents—Bernard and Victoria—who were my very first spiritual teachers. Through the way they parented me, they showed me how to love unconditionally and how to, in the face of the unknown, walk in faith that all is well. I love you both and am grateful and honored to carry on your legacy of love and faith!

contents

two notes on language

Disability Language

Within the disability community, there are two dominant ways we refer to our disability status: identity-first language (i.e., disabled person) and person-first language (i.e., person with a disability). Throughout this book, you will notice that I use both identity-first language and person-first language as well as terms such as "lives with a disability." My reason for using such a wide range of language to describe disability is quite simple: I am a spiritual being having a human incarnation. I am a spirit, not a body. I have a body, but I'm so much more than my right index finger or my left knee or a hair follicle on my scalp. As a spirit, I'm a part of the Divine that is not bound, or defined, by the physical. However, I do understand that my spirit is just one part of me—the most important part, but not the only part. My body is another aspect of my being. I am a spirit who has been given a body to use as a tool.

Thus, I combine my spirit with the experience of living with my body to express the Divine in a way that only I can. I'm a proud member of every category my body fits into: Black, disabled, a woman, an American, on and on. All of these identities have come together to form the lens through which I experience the world that is unique to me and through which I express the Divine. My life with cerebral palsy (CP) has shown me truths such as the strength of the spirit to overcome physical limitations, the need to march in the streets to demand equal rights, and the depth of God's love for me through the presence of continuous miracles. Thus, I use an eclectic body of language to describe disability because my language must reflect the breadth of my lived experience: from the spiritual to the physical. Living with disability is a multifaceted adventure, and any attempt to describe disability requires a plethora of terms.

I understand some people in the disability community only use identity-first language or person-first language. If you staunchly use one or the other, please feel free to imagine that I wrote this book using your preferred disability language.

Use of the Word *God*

I use the word *God* quite a bit throughout this book because this is a book about spirituality, and God is one of the ways I'm most comfortable talking about spirituality. However, I understand that the word *God* can be a trigger for some. If you do not care for, or have an aversion to, the word *God*, I invite you to replace it with any other word that you feel comfortable using as you read this book. God does not care what you call It, and using the word *God* is by no means a prerequisite for having a deep, beautiful spiritual practice. God will respond with equal love, grace, majesty, and power if you call It God, the Divine, the Loving Presence, the Universe, Spirit, or something else. One of the keys to spiritual practice is to acknowledge that there is a loving entity that exists throughout all space and time, that this entity has far greater power than any human being, and that this entity only wants the best for you. As long as you are sincere in your desire to meet It, God does not put restrictions on what It wants to be called. God simply wants you to show up to your relationship with It fully as yourself.

how to use this book

Spirituality and spiritual practices have become more popular and more mainstream than ever before, and at the same time, society has become increasingly inclusive of those with disabilities. However, discussions about how to apply spiritual principles to the lived experience of disability seem elusive, and finding a guide on modifying spiritual practices for those with various disabilities can be challenging. This book aims to remedy both situations.

Since this book is intended to address the experiences and needs of those living with disabilities, a logical question is, "Just who do I include in my definition of disability?" I use an inclusive definition of disability. This book is geared toward those who have visible disabilities, non-apparent disabilities, or both. Those with physical disabilities, intellectual disabilities, cognitive disabilities, chronic illnesses, sensory disabilities, learning disabilities, communication disabilities, psychiatric disabilities, and those who are neurodivergent will find spiritual exercises included in this book that have been modified with their needs in mind.

While there are different ways of understanding spirituality, this book discusses spirituality through the lens of metaphysics. Worry not if you don't have your high-school physics textbook on hand or you never took physics. Metaphysics is not the same as physics. Metaphysics is the science of transcending the physical and teaches us that the solution to any situation experienced in the physical world lies in the spiritual world; we only need to bring the solutions found in the spiritual world to the physical one.

As you may have guessed, according to metaphysics, two worlds exist: the physical world and the spiritual world. Within the physical world, our bodies' senses—sight, touch, smell, sound, and taste—tell us that each person is separate from all other individuals on this planet and that every entity that exists within creation is separate from all other entities, be they planets, animals, stars, flowers, etc. The physical world can seem more real than the spiritual world because the physical is tangible. Depending on our abilities, we can taste, touch, feel, hear, and/or see things in the physical realm. Because of the signals we receive from our senses, it's tempting to disregard the spiritual world and exist only in the physical. However, if we are only aware of, and operate solely in, the physical world, we are cutting ourselves off from the realm of infinite knowledge that is essential to living a full life and solving the "problems" that come our way.

Conversely, within the spiritual world every living being is one with all other beings because we were all created by the same force, which I call God. We are consciously aware of our connection to God and our ability to tap into it. Any challenge that arises in the physical world can be handled by going to the spiritual world. While many believe that the power to handle any situation and to create what we want for ourselves in the physical world must originate from our bodies, brains, material resources, and other physical entities, metaphysics teaches us that the true power to create what we authentically desire resides in the spiritual world and encourages us to engage in spiritual practices that allow us to embody the spiritual world while we reside in the physical one. For when we engage in spiritual practices, we go to the realm of love, solutions, and possibilities and bring those qualities into the physical world, which enable us to anchor all the blessings of the Divine on Earth.

This book will teach you how to become a metaphysician—that is, how to be someone who lives in the physical world but channels and embodies the love, solutions, and possibilities of the spiritual world, regardless of your disability status, over the course of eight chapters. Each chapter focuses on one spiritual practice and includes both a discussion of how that spiritual practice enhances your awareness of your connection to God and a story that demonstrates how I used the spiritual practice to transform a challenging situation into a joyous experience. A section entitled HOW TO features exercises to incorporate the spiritual practice into your life. Most exercises include a description of the traditional way to do the exercise as well as disability-specific modifications. Disability-specific modifications to the exercises can be found in the section entitled ACCESS NOTES.

Since more than one diagnosis can cause the same functional limitation, and in an effort to make sure this book did not become an encyclopedia, I do not list every diagnosis that may benefit from a certain modification to an exercise. Instead, in most chapters, I list a functional limitation and one or more modifications to a given exercise to address the access needs of people with that specific limitation. For example, instead of listing every diagnosis that may cause someone to have limited upper body mobility, I write, "If you have limited upper body mobility, try the following modifications . . ." Thus, when looking for a modification to meet your needs, look for the functional limitation you are trying to address rather than for a specific diagnosis. The one exception to this is the Meditation chapter. This chapter includes modifications that are listed according to both diagnosis and functional limitation.

The exercises in this book fall into one of two categories, either providing step-by-step instructions for how to do a particular practice—such as how to pray an affirmative prayer—or listing actions you can do to create a mindset conducive to experiencing a particular practice—such as surrendering to the Divine.

When reading this book, you can begin with the INTRODUCTION and read straight through to the end, or you can choose to read the chapter about the spiritual practice that most interests you. You will reap the same benefits regardless of which method you choose.

As you build your personal spiritual practice, start slowly. It can be tempting to get excited and want to incorporate as many practices into your life as quickly as possible. However, this can leave you feeling overwhelmed and deciding this whole spirituality thing is for the birds. So, in an effort to help you engage in a committed spiritual practice, and not leave your practice up to the birds in your neighborhood, I recommend that you find one spiritual exercise that piques your interest and try your best to do that one exercise for 14 consecutive days. On your first day, do the exercise for five minutes, at the most. Over the course of the 14 days, slowly increase the amount of time you spend doing the exercise each day until you have reached the maximum amount of time suggested in this book or the maximum amount of time that is healthy for you.

At the end of 14 days, check in with yourself. Do you still enjoy the exercise? Have you noticed a subtle, or not so subtle, change in yourself over the course of the 14 days? Is this something you want to continue doing? If so, determine how often you want to do the exercise each week and record it either in the back of this book or somewhere else. If not, that's okay. Let go of that exercise and try another one.

As you do each exercise, continue reading the book to determine if there are other exercises you want to try. If there are other exercises that interest you, write them down so that when you are ready to try a new exercise, you know exactly what exercise is next on your list.

Once you have found three or four spiritual exercises that you want to continue doing after you have finished reading this book, determine how often you want to do each exercise. You don't need to do every spiritual exercise every day, but I would recommend doing at least one spiritual practice every day, even if you only spend a short time doing the exercise.

Although I include a suggested amount of time to do each exercise, adjust the time you spend engaging in each exercise to fit your unique schedule, lifestyle, and abilities. If you tire easily, then engage in spiritual practice in such a way that you still have the energy and health you need to fulfill your other responsibilities. The goal of spiritual practice is to expand your awareness of your connection with God, not push yourself to ill health in the pursuit of the "ideal" way of doing spiritual practices. So determine a schedule that enables you to consistently engage in your practice *and* stay as healthy as possible for you.

When I started studying *A Course in Miracles* (*ACIM*), I read a chapter in the main text and did one workbook exercise every day, based on my teacher's suggestion. During my second week of study, however, I experienced a sudden and marked increase in the tone in my muscles, which makes them tight and stiff and my movements limited. Although I experience high muscle tone on a regular basis, what I was experiencing then was on a level that I rarely felt. It became so severe that it interfered with my ability to breathe and move from one place to another. This is my body's way of telling me that I am overextending myself, and I knew that for the sake of my safety (and my sanity), I had to stop studying *ACIM*. Once my muscle tone returned to normal, I went back to reading a chapter and doing an exercise from the workbook each day. Once again, the tone in my muscles went through the roof. I began to realize that I wouldn't be able to keep up this schedule and maintain my typical mobility and ability to breathe. Since I'm quite fond of breathing and transferring safely, I decided to read one chapter five days per week and do a workbook exercise three days per week. And guess what? Not only did my muscle tone stay at my normal level while studying *ACIM*, but I also started experiencing more miracles in my life than when I was studying the book every day!

God knows when you are doing your best, so do what you can, and you will reap the same rewards as someone who may have more energy and who spends more time engaging in spiritual practices. The most important thing is that you do your best and you sincerely intend to develop, or deepen, your relationship with the Divine.

If you are not sure which spiritual practice to try first, begin with meditating for 14 consecutive days. I explain how to do Transcendental meditation in the Meditation chapter. After you have been meditating for a few days, ask the following question before one of your meditation sessions: "God, which spiritual practice should I try next?" Begin meditating and remain open to receiving an answer to your question.

Now, I would be remiss if I didn't explain the following phenomenon to you: If you have never engaged in a committed spiritual practice or it's been a while, chances are fairly high that your life will get topsy-turvy when you begin this journey. It can be disconcerting when you notice that your life has become quite unpredictable, but fortunately it will not last forever. Sometimes people think, "Here I am, doing this spirituality thing, and my life has become absolute chaos since I started! Am I doing something wrong?" No, you are not doing anything wrong. In fact, if some things in your life begin to get shaky, you are actually right on schedule for your transformation journey to begin.

When we do not engage in spiritual practice regularly, we shove our feelings about the parts of our lives that have caused us pain or unhappiness into a box within ourselves, like a cardboard box forgotten in the back of a closet labeled: "Stuff I'd Rather Forget." We do our best not to acknowledge whatever is in that box. Some of us pretend that we don't have such a box and that everything is fine, nudging it back into the dark and dusty corners of our minds. Others become so good at not acknowledging the box that they become oblivious to the impact of its contents. Either way, we don't allow ourselves to feel whatever emotions are tucked away in the box, and we are unaware of just how unhappy we are with certain situations.

The longer we live without seeking conscious connection with the Divine, the more emotional junk we stuff into that box. Once you begin engaging in a spiritual practice, however, you open yourself up to the Divine that is within you. This means that God finds a way to the back of any internal closets that you have filled with boxes of unprocessed emotions, opens up every single box, and fills the entire space with love and light. All the junk that you stuffed into those boxes comes tumbling out, spilling across the floor like a pile of old love letters or photos from a hard time in your life as if to say, "If you're going to fully embrace the love of who you are, we can no longer stay inside of you." Here all the unhappy feelings you stuffed into the boxes come to the forefront for you to feel. And all of those less-than-desirable situations in your life that you chose to be unaware of, or to settle for, come rushing into your awareness and become so uncomfortable that you are forced to transform the situations.

When we experience our lives going all topsy-turvy, what is really happening is that anything not in alignment with the flow of God is coming to the surface, creating an opportunity for you to recognize and transform it.

God is love, joy, happiness, and truth. Anything that is a part of your life that does not engender those feelings will be brought to your attention so that they can be addressed and transformed. Harmony and disharmony cannot co-exist within one person. So, the more time you spend in communion with God, the more you will begin to recognize those things that cause disharmony in your life and the better you will become at working with the Divine to transmute those things. You will no longer need that battered old box to hide your pain, because you will have the strength to face it.

So, what do you do if this happens to you? Continue to build your spiritual practice. Know that this too shall pass, and the life waiting for you on the other side is so worth the discomfort you are feeling right now. Be very gentle with yourself. Treat yourself to your favorite food or hobby, or let yourself sleep in a little for a few days. Practice excellent self-care. Drink more water than you normally do for a few days. If you are tube fed and can safely increase your water intake, give yourself an extra flush of any amount that is healthy for you. If you cannot increase your water intake, take an extra-long shower or bath for a few days. Be open to releasing anyone or anything that needs to be released. Ask trusted family and friends to support you in whatever way you need. Above all else, trust in the love that is trying to help you give birth to the life of your dreams.

Finally, and most importantly, have fun! Living in conscious connection with the Divine is fun, exciting, miraculous, awe-inspiring, and sometimes even absolutely hilarious. God is all good things, which means God is joy, bliss, ecstasy, and unfathomable blessings, and God wants us to experience these things. Bring a lighthearted curiosity to your practice. Know that God only wants for you what your soul wants for itself, so buckle up for the ride of a lifetime with your soul in the driver's seat!

introduction

I was born blue, lifeless, and with significant brain damage. Due to my traumatic birth, I use a wheelchair, have limited use of my hands and arms, and work hard to speak clearly. As a result of my dedication to spiritual practice, I have earned a Ph.D. in economics from MIT, acted in film, and worked with organizations to improve the lives of disabled people around the world.

Spirituality Is for Every Body reveals how I turned my diagnosis of cerebral palsy into my prognosis of a joyous life fueled by an ever-evolving and deepening awareness of my connection with the Divine.

I am one of the millions of people who lives with at least one disability. In 2023, the Centers for Disease Control and Prevention (CDC) website estimated that 26 percent of adults in the United States have a disability, making those with disabilities the largest minority group in the country.[1] Living with a disability can be challenging beyond simply dealing with the disability itself and can lead to increased medical costs and complications, social stigma, isolation, depression, and the all-too-common question, "Am I enough?" hitting that much harder. Studies have shown that over 80 percent of disabled American adults indicate that spirituality is the foundation of how they cope with their disability. People with disabilities who engage in spiritual practices like praying, reading religious texts, attending weekly religious services, or meditating on a regular basis have a stronger sense of purpose, better health outcomes, and experience less depression compared to those who do not have a spiritual life.[2] Given the many benefits of engaging in spirituality, the desire of disabled people and their families to receive instruction from clergy on how to apply spirituality to disability-specific experiences is not just understandable, but essential.[3]

However, the vast majority of disabled people and their families do not receive such instruction for two reasons. First, simply attending church can be prohibitively difficult for the disabled and their families. Fifty-five percent of people with disabilities cannot attend church due to barriers such as inaccessible church buildings and a lack of accessible transportation.[4] According to one study, nearly ⅓ of 400 families who had someone with a newly diagnosed disability left their church within one year of the diagnosis because of an unwelcoming atmosphere, such as other parishioners making unkind comments about the family member's disability and church staff being unwilling to provide accommodations so that the disabled individual can fully participate in church activities.[5] Second, the majority of disabled people who attend church are unlikely to have a minister educated on how to apply spiritual principles to disability because fewer than 10 percent of seminaries offer a single class on the subject.[6] These realities leave many people with disabilities on their own to figure out how to apply spirituality to their life experience.

My goal with this book is to help people with disabilities find inspiration, gain confidence, and learn skills to deepen their connection to God in their own way. By reading engaging, funny, and sometimes unfathomable stories from my life, readers will see just how spirituality can help disabled people live incredible lives *with* their disabilities. Seeing how I have applied spiritual principles and practices to situations unique to disability will empower disabled people and their families to do the same. Doing the exercises included in each chapter will enable each reader to develop their own spiritual practice. Unlike any other book that gives people spiritual exercises based on metaphysical principles, I explain how the reader can modify each exercise based on the reader's disability.

I am the perfect person to share this book with the world. Disabled since birth, I have been an active member of the disability community from the day I was diagnosed with cerebral palsy. As a child and teenager, I attended schools and camps for disabled children, worked as a camp counselor for disabled campers, and served as a peer counselor to disabled high school students. As an adult, I attend national and international conferences for those working in the field of disability policy, I counsel parents and guardians of disabled children, and I mentor disabled college students and disabled young professionals. My substantive experience with the disability community means I understand not only my disability and its impacts, but also the abilities and needs of those with other disabilities and their families. For me, disability is intimate, a blessing, and something that I have navigated with my family and friends for decades. I know the joys and pains that come with living with disability. I love the disability community and want to do all I can to help every member of the community live in the full beauty of the Divine.

Just as I have been active in the disability community for most of my life, I have studied spirituality and spiritual practice since early childhood. As a child, I attended churches where the ministers and lay leaders taught me that I was perfect as I was and loved fully by God. In college, I began studying metaphysics, spirituality, and spiritual practice by reading copious books. In my early 30s, I expanded my studies of these topics by enrolling in classes where I studied with leading teachers of metaphysics and spirituality. During each class, I learned spiritual theory and practice, and I asked my teachers how each practice could be modified for those with various abilities. After taking several classes, I began using my knowledge of spirituality and spiritual practices to help my friends with various disabilities deepen their awareness of their connection with the Divine. As a result of these sessions, I learned which modifications work best, and I witnessed firsthand the growth in confidence and joy that comes with engaging in spiritual practices that are tailored to one's unique abilities.

This book aligns with the current mores, desires, and goals of the disability community. To become more inclusive of marginalized disabled people, the disability community recently adopted the Disability Justice Movement (DJM), which is a framework for disability advocacy that seeks to understand the experiences of disabled women and disabled people of color, among others.[7] As a result, many with disabilities are seeking to learn about the lives of disabled women and disabled people of color so that the experiences of these groups can be fully incorporated into disability culture and advocacy. Since this book discusses my life experiences as a disabled Black woman, it provides information that is in demand by the disability community. Additionally, the DJM seeks the full inclusion of disabled people and disability issues into mainstream culture. It is my hope that since spirituality is a part of mainstream culture, and this book demonstrates how to incorporate disability issues into spiritual conversations and teaches how to include the disabled in spiritual practices, *Spirituality Is for Every Body* will help achieve the disability community's desire to be fully included as valuable and valued members of society with cultural relevance and influence.

In this book, you will find a practical guide for how to apply spiritual principles to disability-related issues and how to adapt spiritual practices for people with various disabilities. It expands the discussion of the benefits of spirituality to be inclusive of the experiences of the disability community, thereby providing a resource for not just coping with disability, but thriving with disability.

CHAPTER ONE

surrender

***Surrendering my life to God is the ultimate taking of personal responsibility, as God is not outside but within us.*[1]**

— MARIANNE WILLIAMSON

One of my most vivid memories of Sunday School was being taught that I needed to surrender my life to God. This lesson is so vivid because I heard it often, and before I understood it, the idea of surrendering to God absolutely terrified me! Seven-year-old Allison believed that surrendering to God meant I would have to give up all of my most cherished worldly possessions—including my toys, extensive collection of nail polish, and clothes—and go live on the top of a mountain in a remote land. All I would eat was gruel, and I'd have to wear a robe made out of a burlap potato sack and no shoes. I had an active imagination, and my imagination told me that surrendering to God would be no fun.

As a child, the vast majority of artwork that I saw of God depicted Him as a white man sitting in the clouds with a stern look on His face. God always seemed to be looking down on humans and passing judgment on every single one of us. That artwork led me to believe that God was a single entity that was outside of me. Yes, God loved me, but those images instilled in me the belief that there was only one God and only one way to please Him. Hence, I believed that surrendering to God had to look one way regardless of whether or not that one way would bring me happiness.

As a young child, I didn't fully understand that God is actually within me and that there are as many faces of God as there are sentient beings on the planet. God wants only what will bring me authentic joy and wants me to experience things that will enable me to fully express the glory of the deepest part of my being. Since God is all-knowing, It knows what will bring each one of us true joy, and It knows just how to orchestrate events in our lives so that we experience what we most desire.

Our role in experiencing the things that will bring us bliss is to surrender spiritually. In Western culture, however, the word *surrender* does not have the best connotation and is often interpreted as giving up or somehow relinquishing your power because you are not strong enough to win. But, as Roger Gabriel writes for Chopra.com, when you surrender to God, you are "stepping out of all limitations, expanding beyond your usual conditioning, and opening to infinite possibilities."[2] For in surrendering to God, we open ourselves—our mind, our heart, our spirit—to the love, intelligence, beauty, and blessings of the Most High.

Surrendering to God means relinquishing control by dropping our human notions of what should or shouldn't be and allowing God to lead the way. Once we relinquish control and completely open ourselves to the Divine, we expand our receptivity to the goodness of God. Through this expanded receptivity, Divine resources, such as creativity and insights, become increasingly active in our lives and guide us on our journey, which allows us to realize our dreams—both known and unknown.

Although surrendering spiritually is teeming with gifts and unimaginable joy, surrendering to God, when you are not quite sure of what or who God is, can be a tall order. Along the same lines, some people have been taught that God is vindictive, metes out punishment to "sinners," and engages in less-than-savory behaviors. Surrendering to such a God would be scary for anyone. I understand that some religions believe in this type of God; however, the God that I know, that I study, and that I have built a relationship with my entire life is pure love. Surrendering requires trusting in the love, grace, and blessings of God. After all, who is going to voluntarily surrender to something that might annihilate them or cause them to experience misfortune? Such an act of surrender would go against humanity's instinct to seek self-preservation. Hence, learning the true nature of God is a key part of the surrendering process.

As an adult, after studying God deeply and understanding God in a way I never had as a frightened child, I was finally able to surrender to God enough to receive an answer to a lifelong, deeply personal question.

Ever since I was a little girl, I firmly believed that I was meant to have cerebral palsy (CP) and I was meant to improve the lives of people with disabilities. I attribute this firm belief to two complementary phenomena.

First, as my maternal grandmother, and several other adults in my life, would often say, "Allison has an old soul."

The first time I heard my grandmother say it, I asked my mom what it meant. "How could I be old if I was just a kid?" I asked.

My mom chuckled and said, "You're not old. You are very wise. People who have old souls are just wise beyond their age."

I understood that, but I was a bit incredulous. I thought every six-year-old dreamed about making the world more accessible to people who couldn't walk or talk or hear and told everyone who would listen. And surely, I wasn't the only nine-year-old who entered an essay contest about what programs I would put on my radio station and used that essay to discuss the need to include disabled people in the medium to create a more equitable society. Only as a teenager did I learn that while most kids had the same favorite cartoons I had, usually their favorite books featured those cartoon characters too, whereas, my favorite book was *Meet Martin Luther King, Jr.*

When I was in the first grade, I was interviewed by my local PBS station. During the interview, I was asked why I liked that book. Six-year-old me replied that I liked it because "he fought for our rights." The deep wisdom within my soul came into this world knowing that I was meant to have CP and use my life to advance the rights of those with disabilities in the same way that Dr. King fought for the rights of Black Americans.

The second phenomenon perfectly dovetails with the first: from the time I was four years old, the adults in my life gave me opportunities to, and nurtured my love of, advocating for the disability community. I went to a school for disabled children from nursery school through the second grade. During the school day, teachers encouraged my classmates and me to advocate for ourselves and to view ourselves as capable young people who just did things a bit differently from others.

When I was four years old, the staff of the school began asking my parents if I could make appearances at various events and give interviews about the importance of extracurricular and academic programs for disabled children. Since I was just four years old when I started, I'm not sure how profound my answers were. But I loved telling people about the abilities my friends and I had, not just the disabilities, and that more things should be accessible to us no matter what our disability was.

While these opportunities were great fun for me, given my age, my parents had to take time off work and coordinate their schedules so that I could participate in all of this advocacy. My parents were young professionals with demanding jobs, active civic and social lives, a marriage, and two young daughters to care for. They were incredibly busy, but they also had a daughter who was being asked to speak on behalf of her community.

When I was five years old, my parents decided to have "The Talk" . . . "The Allison Advocacy Talk," that is. My parents were receiving so many requests for me to advocate that they had to decide how to handle it. They agreed that if my voice could help improve the opportunities and equality of the disability community, they wanted me to use that voice. They decided that, as long as I wanted to speak, they'd commit to getting me to all the advocacy engagements I was invited to.

These two facts of my life—my early call to advocacy and my supportive family and community—coalesced to create a vision of myself as a person who had a mission that could only be fulfilled with the body that I was in. I deeply enjoyed advocating for my community and was proud to have CP. I welcomed the opportunity to talk to anyone, anytime, about disability and all the things that those with disabilities are able to do, as long as I wasn't busy riding my Big Wheel or on the verge of eating a Rice Krispies Treat. Even though I loved advocacy, I was still a kid.

You may think that given these experiences, I never questioned the CP. But I did. Even though I always believed that I was meant to have CP, occasionally, I wondered if I was deluding myself. If I was simply "making the best out of the situation," and that the CP was a mistake or an accident.

While living with a disability is beautiful because you appreciate things on a level that is different from many without disabilities, and you see humanity and ability in ways that are unique to the disability experience, it can also be painful, physically and emotionally, and sometimes so difficult that you wonder where you'll get the strength to keep going.

Every now and then, questions such as, "Where was God at the time of birth? Where was God when the umbilical cord was so tightly wound around my neck that I was deprived of oxygen for precious minutes? Why, God, did you not keep my heart rate just high enough to prevent the damage to my brain? Was I not important enough to protect?" would find their way into my otherwise happy, sunshine-filled thoughts.

Fortunately, these thoughts came quite rarely. But the thing is, when these questions came, I didn't have any concrete answers. I just had my deeply held belief that I was created to fulfill a mission that could only be accomplished with this body. However, I wanted to have more than a belief system. I wanted answers to my questions. As a teenager, I simply couldn't find those answers.

Once I became a young adult, though, answers started popping into my awareness. Throughout my 20s, I increased the number of spiritual practices I did each day, and I increased the amount of time I spent doing each practice. When I turned 20, I meditated almost every day for between 15 and 30 minutes, and I attended church occasionally. By the time I was 29 years old, I meditated every day, prayed every morning and evening, and engaged in a weekly gratitude practice. As a result, my alignment with the Divine grew because the time I spent actively and consciously connecting with the Divine grew. This increased alignment meant that I began to have these little pinpricks of understanding about the circumstances surrounding my birth. I still didn't have all the answers I sought, but by the time I entered my 30s, I began having regular epiphanies. One of my biggest epiphanies helped me understand just why I had to be rushed to a different hospital within minutes of my birth. I was so excited when I had this revelation that I shared it with my dad.

"You know, Dad, I realized that the night I was born, I was just letting you and mom know who I was!" I said during one of our Saturday afternoon phone calls.

"Tell me more," my dad said, intrigued.

"Well, when have you ever known me to do anything like everyone else?"

"Never," my dad said, chuckling. "You always do everything with your own flair!"

"Right! So, why on Earth would I be born in a quiet, sedate manner like most people? That's simply not me. If I was going to be born, the world was going to know that a little one named Allison Victoria Thompkins had officially entered the building! Lights were going to be flashing!

Sirens were going to be blaring to announce my birth! Dad, do you realize that I literally stopped traffic from the moment I was born?" I said, referring to the ambulance ride that rushed me from the hospital where I was born to a hospital across town that specialized in treating infants in critical condition. "If that's not being born with a flair, I don't know what is!"

I continued, "Plus, you know my love of speed."

"Oh yes! Your mom and I know just how much you like to go as fast as you can in *everything* you do!"

"So, it makes complete sense that my very first ride in a vehicle was in an ambulance going at top speed through the city."

While I was beginning to piece together the parallels between my personality and the events following my birth, I still didn't fully understand the events of my birth and just how God fit into them. I had yet to develop a deep enough understanding of, and alignment with, God to receive the answers that I most wanted. So, I still relied on my belief system from childhood that insisted that I had CP because I had a mission that could only be fulfilled with this body.

As I entered my 30s, I began studying *A Course in Miracles,* which is a book that teaches spiritual principles from a metaphysical perspective, and attending Agape International Spiritual Center, a church that teaches the metaphysics of spirituality. I had gone to church for years before this and attended Bible study classes, but it wasn't until these two events, which were monumental in my journey to understanding God better, that I began to understand various spiritual principles on a more profound level. The spiritual principles that I thought I had understood all my life, I now felt in my very being. I was raised to believe that God loved me, and I believed It did, but I began to *feel* God's love for me in a way I never had before. The concepts that I had been taught in church for years had finally made the trip from my mind to my heart. I felt more connected with God than I ever had before. I understood the Divine in a way I never had before.

As my understanding of God and spirituality evolved due to studying spirituality more and engaging in more spiritual practices than ever before in my life, I became open to having a new understanding of CP. In fact, I wanted a concrete, deep-seated knowing about the CP. I no longer wanted to rely on the belief system I had constructed for myself in childhood. I was no longer a child. I was an adult who wanted to replace the belief system of my childhood with an unwavering knowing of an adult who has a deep, committed relationship with God. I wanted an understanding of CP that spoke to me as a 30-something who studied quantum physics and energy healing, and who understood many principles of God, but who was having some difficulty reconciling the power, compassion, and the love of God with the events of my birth. I wanted to know once and for all, "God, what happened and why?" This desire rolled around in my mind, heart, and spirit for quite a while as I continued to work and wait.

One evening, I was relaxing in bed, and I had just finished one of my favorite activities: watching tennis. At the conclusion of the match, I turned off the television and had a sudden inspired thought: if I wanted a direct realization, all I had to do was ask the Divine.

So, I asked. I didn't say a word. I simply thought, "God, can you please give me clarity about the events of my birth? I just want to understand what happened and why."

As soon as I thought the word *why*, I was transported to another place in my mind. Although my body was still in my bedroom, I no longer saw my bedroom. All I saw was space, outer space, from what I could tell. God was there in the form of a thin, flat membrane. This membrane looked like a transparent flat sheet of a bed. The God membrane extended in every direction . . . forever. God was everywhere you looked for as far as the eye could see. I was there too, but I didn't have a body. I was a ball of energy that was a part of the membrane that was God. I was literally a part of God.

Beneath God, was Earth. There was a spotlight shining on a delivery room. My mom was on the delivery table, trying to birth me into the world. My dad was standing just behind her, willing me to be born.

Fortunately, I didn't see what they were wearing at the time. My parents were dedicated to the fashion of the 1970s, so I cannot tell you the number of times that they've shown me pictures of themselves as young adults and I cried out, while shaking my head in utter disbelief, "Did you really have to wear polyester, plaid bell bottoms? Weren't there any other options?" So, you see, God knows everything we can handle, and what we can't . . . even the small stuff.

What I did see were the doctors and nurses rushing around the delivery room, trying to figure out how to save this little infant that was meant to be me. The God membrane was also in the room, stretching from outer space into the delivery room. God was wrapped around my mother's head, wrapped around my father's shoulders, wrapped around the hands of the doctor delivering me and inside my mother's womb. God was everywhere at once. Although I was still a part of God in space and didn't have a body, I could see the events unfolding in the delivery room. I could see the worry on the faces of the doctor and nurses as the vital signs of baby me deteriorated. I could see my mother going into prayer as the situation became increasingly dire. I could see the love and strength my father was pouring into my mother as he stood by her side, literally and figuratively.

Yet the ball of energy that was me, my spirit, was still firmly fixed in God in outer space. I was quite cozy up there. I was ready to stay with God as a ball of energy and just watch the events unfold.

However, God spoke to me, spirit me, and said, "This is for you," and motioned to the scene below. Spirit me "looked" at the events below, and decided to stay put, to stay with the Creator of all.

However, God repeated, "This is what I have for you to do. This is for you," and motioned again to the delivery room.

Spirit me moved a wee bit, but conveyed to God that the events we were watching looked like a hot mess, so I was just fine and dandy to stay where I was. God, however, was not deterred.

God replied, "This is what I have for you to do. This is yours. I am with you always, but this is yours to do."

Spirit me took one last long look at the events unfolding on Earth, took a moment to soak up the Godliness of God, and began to roll down the God membrane—just like a child going down a slide—right into my mother's womb.

As soon as spirit me entered my mom's womb, the vision ended, and I was back in my bedroom in the present day, but with an entirely different understanding of my birth, myself, cerebral palsy, and most of all, God. I didn't know what to think or even how to conceptualize what I had just experienced. I was excited, in awe, overjoyed, tremendously grateful, and on the verge of tears all at once for the gift I had just received. Not knowing what to do with everything I was feeling, I just sat still. I wanted to hold on to the feeling of being one with God for as long as possible.

Then I realized, "Oh my goodness! I'm exactly who I am meant to be. I was meant to have CP. God knew exactly what was happening, and my spirit was chosen specifically for this body! OH MY GOODNESS!"

I thanked God profusely for the insight, the knowledge, and the revelation of the spiritual story of my birth. I now knew—like I knew my name—that God was in fact present at my birth. And not only was God present, but It orchestrated every single aspect of my birth, including what spirit was chosen to breathe life into this body that would have CP. Far from CP being an accident or something that happened that we now have to make the best of, God showed me that It created my experience of CP. God knew the plans It had for my body and my life. Those plans could be fulfilled only if my body was born with athetoid CP, and athetoid CP comes about only after a specific series of events.

Furthermore, not only was I held in God's love during my birth, so were my parents. Like many parents, mine had planned on having a delivery conducive to a baby being born without CP; however, that was not God's plan. God had to get in there and rebel rouse a bit. God had to create the physical conditions aligned with my body having CP. We humans have free will, which means my parents had many choices of how to handle the unfolding events of my birth. They could have become fearful, angry, bitter, or untrusting in God. They could have turned their backs on God, given up on the possibility of me being born alive, and missed the opportunity to have the grace of God fulfill the Divine mission of my birth.

When we're experiencing a challenging time, it is tempting to believe that God isn't present. That if God was present, the tough time somehow would not exist. My vision, however, showed me that sometimes we will just experience challenging times, not because God isn't present, but because those challenges are critical for the realization of God's plan. And God is in fact with us in the midst of the challenge. God loves us, and while that love may not prevent every challenging experience, it does provide a way to ease us through the situation. If we allow ourselves to remain one with the Divine presence, we create the environment for the Divine purpose of that challenge to come to fruition.

God was cradling my mother's head, whispering to her to pray in the midst of the seeming chaos, and giving her the strength to birth me even though the birthing process was 180 degrees away from what she planned on, and the courage to embark on the journey of mothering me to fulfill my God-given mission. God was wrapped around my father's shoulders, shoring him up and steadying him and giving him strength as he embarked on the journey of being my father and not knowing what that meant. He only knew that I came out of my mother's womb, blue and silent. God was there with them in the midst of that challenge.

And my parents decided to focus on the presence of God. My parents began to pray the moment my life was in peril. They focused single-mindedly on God's grace to help me survive the delivery even when that outcome was in doubt. By their faith in God, they magnified the presence of God within themselves, which pulled the will of God into that delivery room and ushered me, CP and all, into the world.

Before the night I saw this vision, I sometimes wondered if God temporarily abdicated Its throne during my birth to go do Its nails or perhaps get a latte. However, I knew now that God was the energy that created and fueled my birth and that, once I was born, smiled at the perfect unfolding of Its Divine plan. Oh, what a gift it is to surrender! I went from being slightly uncertain about the presence of CP in my life to knowing on the deepest, most profound level that I was created just as God designed me!

Now, you may be wondering, "Allison, why did it take you 30-something years to get that answer? Why in the name of good gravy didn't you ask for clarity before?" Well, the truth is, I did. But I had to change one thing within me before I could receive the answer to my prayer. I had to surrender to God.

Previously, I received complete answers about the events *following* my birth, but I had not received answers about the birth itself—the answers I most wanted—because when I asked God questions about how the CP came about before this night, I wanted the answer to fit into the box of what I believed was an appropriate answer. Truth be told, I was scared. What if I found out that the CP was a massive cosmic mistake? Or, what if I was informed that CP served absolutely no purpose and I had deluded myself into thinking I was meant to make a difference in this world? Sure, it would have been a delusion that I committed to fully, and I had done some pretty cool things as a result, but my very understanding of myself would have been rocked to its core. What it all boiled down to was I did not fully trust in the All-Loving Presence before this night. I hadn't fully surrendered yet.

I was open to asking the question, but I was wedded to what the answer had to be. Since I wanted God's answer to meet my understanding of disability, I was too invested in being told the "right" answer. When we cling to our expectations of how God should answer our prayers, we move ourselves out of alignment with God because we constrict God.

God is indivisible and infinite. God does not divide Itself up or show up anywhere small. That would go against the very nature of God. Hence, if we ask God a question but are not open to receiving the full answer—the full truth—we won't receive an answer. In fact, we *can't* receive an answer because God, by Its very nature, cannot give partial truths. It cannot fit into our small understanding of the world, nor can It give us only part of an answer—the part we want to hear. We must expand our understanding of God by engaging in spiritual practices so that we have such faith in how much God loves us that we completely open ourselves to God. Only when we completely surrender our minds and our hearts to whatever the truth is, do we provide the room for God to show up fully as Itself and give us the complete, Divine, and absolutely beautiful answer It has for us.

Surrendering to God may mean different things to different people, and it may mean different things to the same person at different times in their life. For some, surrendering to God means releasing control of what they believe is the best course of action and allowing the Divine to reveal to them the best course. For others, surrendering could mean deciding to live the life they have always wanted but are scared to try. For some, they may have surrendered to

God in most areas of their lives but haven't surrendered in other areas.

Regardless of how you may want or need to surrender, spiritual surrendering is simply accepting the current situation as it is instead of trying to force the situation to be different. Eckhart Tolle describes surrender as "the simple but profound wisdom of yielding to rather than opposing the flow of life."[3] Yielding to the flow of life, which is the flow of the Divine, enables us to become aligned with the flow of God. Now, we may not like what is happening, or we may think that if we just push harder or work harder, we can change the circumstances into something more palatable. However, that pushing and straining against what is only pushes us away from God, because God is in the present. God is in the right here and right now. So, pushing the right here and right now away is pushing the power of God away and replacing it with human power, which is never a winning proposition. So, what do you do? Surrender. Accept the situation. Release the belief that you know a better solution. Release the fear of what may happen if you surrender control of the circumstances. In short, decide to have faith that God loves you, allow your thinking mind to step out of the way, and give God space to show up.

Now, I'm not talking about throwing up your hands and saying, "Fine, God. I give up! You do it all." That is not surrendering. This is throwing a temper tantrum and sitting on the sidelines of your life. Surrendering is saying, "Okay, God. I have absolutely no idea of how to get myself to where I truly want to be. And sometimes, I don't even know where I truly want to be. So, I choose to accept where I am and ask you to show me what I need to know to experience true fulfillment." You see, surrender is getting out of the way so we can follow God's lead. Far from giving up, surrendering spiritually is acting from the wisdom, intelligence, and love of the Divine.

HOW TO SURRENDER

Exercises and Prompts

While surrendering to God is filled with gifts and unimaginable joy, it may initially sound a bit daunting, or even scary, because you might be unclear on just what you are surrendering to. If God or spirituality is completely, or mostly, unknown to you, your first step in surrendering to God is to understand and believe in the truth of God. Without understanding or believing in the truth that God intends only the best for you, surrendering to God will, at best, be a struggle and, at worst, simply won't happen. The exercises in this section are divided into three categories based on your comfort level with surrendering: exercises for those who don't know how to or are ambivalent about surrendering, exercises for those who want to go deeper in their surrender practices, and exercises regardless of your comfort level.

If you want to surrender but don't know how, or you are ambivalent about the whole concept of surrendering, I suggest the following two exercises.

Exercise 1: Acquaint yourself with the qualities of God.

a. Review the list of 26 qualities of God below, and choose three qualities that resonate with you:

Abundance	Kindness
Beauty	Limitless
Compassion	Love
Creativity	Oneness
Ease	Organization
Eternal	Peace
Freedom	Perfection
Generosity	Power
Harmony	Truth
Health	Universal
Infinite	Unwavering
Intelligence	Wholeness
Joy	Wisdom

b. Go in front of a mirror or on an app on your mobile device that reflects your image back to you. As you look into your eyes say the following mantra out loud: **"God is [Quality #1]. God is [Quality #2]. God is [Quality #3]."** Say it three times in the morning and three times at night. Do this exercise with the same three qualities for between five and seven days.

c. Then, choose three more qualities and repeat the process.

d. To increase the effectiveness of this exercise, you can repeat the mantra throughout your day, either silently or verbally, in addition to saying the mantra in the morning and the evening. You can also focus on the same qualities for more than seven days.

Exercise 2: Cultivate the energy of surrendering to God within yourself.

a. Go in front of your mirror or on an app on your device that reflects your image back to you and say the following mantra three times in the morning and three times in the evening while looking into your eyes: **"I am open to the possibility of surrendering to God."** To add more power to the words, gently tap on the middle of your collarbone with your fingers as you say the statement. Repeat this exercise until you can say and think the mantra without feeling tension or resistance in your body or mind. This may take a few days, a few weeks, or longer. Just take your time and go at your own pace.

b. Once you can comfortably say that you are open to the possibility of surrendering, say the following three times in the morning and three times in the evening while looking into your eyes: **"I am open to surrendering to God."** To increase the effectiveness of this exercise, gently tap on the middle of your collarbone with your fingers as you say the statement. Say this mantra to yourself until you can say and think it without feeling tension or resistance.

c. Lastly, say the following three times in the morning and three times in the evening while looking into your eyes: **"I surrender to God."** For increased power, gently tap on the middle of your collarbone with your fingers as you say the statement. You can say this mantra to

> yourself until you can say and think it without feeling tension or resistance. Saying this mantra can be a part of your daily spiritual practice for as long as you like.

A note on the aforementioned mantras: Each time you begin saying a mantra that reflects a greater openness to surrendering to God, you may feel uncomfortable or like you don't really feel that way at all. This is okay and normal. When you begin saying a mantra that reflects what you want to embody but don't currently embody, you are stretching your mind, your heart, and your spiritual muscles. This is similar to beginning a new stretching regimen for your physical muscles. You may feel some discomfort or uneasiness when you begin, but this is a sign of your spiritual expansion. Keep at it. You will become more flexible and open with time.

Those who are comfortable surrendering to God can do the following exercise to go deeper in their surrender practice.

Exercise 3: Meditate on surrendering more deeply.

Prepare yourself to meditate. If you want to meditate without a mantra, do the following. Before beginning your meditation, think to yourself, "God, please help me to more deeply surrender to the Divine." Release the thought and go into your meditation. Be receptive to any messages you might receive during your meditation or in the days after your meditation that show you how to surrender deeper.

If you want to meditate using a mantra: you can use the mantra "Surrender to God" or simply "Surrender."

Regardless of how comfortable you are with the concept of surrendering to God, reading about God's goodness and the benefits of surrendering to God—in books like this one and *A Return to Love* by Marianne Williamson—will create an energy within you and around you of surrendering, which will get you into the flow of surrendering.

Exercise 4: Read. Read. Read.

If you want to read something on a daily, or weekly, basis, I recommend reading the following passage either aloud or silently. The passage is an excerpt from *A Parenthesis in Eternity* by Joel S. Goldsmith. Please know that you can change the gender/pronouns in the excerpt below to reflect who you are.

> *Man is an heir of God and entitled to all that the Father has—all the joy, all the abundance, all the infinity, all the life, all the love, and all the wisdom. Man is entitled to every bit of it, and it is being revealed unto him for his use, his joy, his beauty, that his life may be one of Grace and peace. When this is understood, we can then take the next step and realize, "I am that man; I am that being for whom all of this has been created."*
>
> *To each of us will come whatever fulfills his nature. To me, the principles of mathematics and science will not come because that would not fulfill my particular nature. To me come the secrets of the spiritual universe . . . because that fulfills me. In that, I*

find my joy. . . . But then there are others from whom mathematics, chemistry, the arts and sciences will come because these will fulfill their nature.

God is infinite, and we are infinite in being. There is an infinity of nature on Earth, and each one of us has some part in that nature. . . . It is all here for us, and we are so great in God's eyes that he has stored it up for us, that we may know infinite and boundless good.

ACCESS NOTES

Exercise 1: Acquaint yourself with the qualities of God.

1. *If you have difficulty looking into a mirror or an app that shows your image due to the nature of your disability, or you are Deafblind and speak verbally,* memorize the mantra you want to say or have the mantra available to you in another format as you do this exercise. Close your eyes, place both of your hands over your heart, and say the mantra aloud.
2. *If you would like to do this exercise by saying each sentence out loud and you are d/Deaf or hard of hearing,* feel free to sign the sentences if sign language is your preferred language.
3. *If you are Deafblind and communicate via sign language,* memorize the mantra you want to sign or have the mantra accessible to you as you do the exercise. You can do this exercise in one of two ways. Try both ways and determine which one feels best to you.

a. First Method: Begin by closing your eyes and placing one hand over your heart. Next, use your other hand to sign each sentence.

b. Second Method: Begin by closing your eyes. Place both of your hands over your heart. Take a deep, slow breath in and slowly exhale. When you finish exhaling, sign the first sentence. After you sign the sentence, place both of your hands over your heart and take a slow, deep breath. Once you finish that breath, sign the second sentence. When you finish the sentence, place both of your hands over your heart and take another slow, deep breath. Once you finish that breath, sign the final sentence. Place your hands over your heart and take a few deep breaths.

4. *If you can speak but saying the mantra three times in the morning and three times in the evening is not possible,* say the mantra as many times as is healthy for you.
5. *If you are nonverbal, nonspeaking, or minimally verbal,* there are two ways that you can modify this exercise. If you're unsure of which method to try, try both and determine which one feels better to you. Also, know that you can do either method depending on what works best at that time.

a. First, instead of verbally saying the sentences, say the mantra in your mind while you look at yourself in a mirror or app.

b. Second, either have your augmentative and alternative communication (AAC) device or another person speak the mantra while you look at your reflection. If you have another person speak the mantra, ask the person to say your name instead of saying the pronoun "I."

Exercise 2: Cultivate the energy of surrendering to God within yourself.

6. *If you would like to tap on your collarbone while saying the mantras and you do not have the upper body mobility to do so,* try these modifications.

   a. First, if you can physically tap your own collarbone but have a disability that impacts your hands, try the following modifications.

   i. If you have partial use of your hands, you can tap on your collarbone using any part of your hand. If you can tap your collarbone with a closed fist, go for it.

   ii. If you do not have hands or cannot tap with your hands, feel free to tap with whatever body part (such as your wrist or foot), or assistive device, that works for you.

   b. Second, you can imagine that you are tapping your collarbone with your hand as you say the mantra.

   c. Third, you can ask a trusted friend or family member to tap your collarbone for you.

7. *If you would like to tap on your collarbone while saying the mantras and you have bones that fracture easily, or you bruise easily, or you have skin that is easily irritated or damaged,* consult your medical team to see if one of the following modifications is safe for you.

    a. First, lightly place your hand on your collarbone, using the amount of pressure that is healthy for you (this can range from no pressure to very light pressure) and keep your hand on your collarbone for the duration of the exercise.

    b. Second, imagine yourself tapping your collarbone while saying the mantras.

8. *If you would like to tap your collarbone and sign language is your first language,* there are two ways to modify this exercise. You can do either one of the following. If you're unsure of which one to try, do both and determine which one feels better to you.

    a. First, tap on your collarbone with one hand and sign the mantra with your other hand.

    b. Second, you can say the mantra in your head while tapping your collarbone.

9. *If you have difficulty looking at your image in a mirror or on an app due to the nature of your disability, or you are Deafblind and speak verbally,* memorize the mantras you want to say or have the mantras available to you in another format as you do this exercise. Close your eyes, place both of your hands over

your heart, and say the mantras aloud. If you would like to tap your collarbone, tap your collarbone instead of putting your hands over your heart.

10. *If you are Deafblind and communicate via sign language,* begin by closing your eyes. Place both of your hands over your heart. Take a slow, deep breath. When you finish one deep breath, sign the following mantra three times: "I completely surrender to God." When you finish signing the sentence three times, place both of your hands over your heart and take another slow, deep breath. If you would like to tap your collarbone, tap your collarbone while saying the sentences in your head.
11. *If you can speak but saying the mantra three times in the morning and three times in the evening is not possible,* say the mantra as many times as is healthy for you.
12. *If you are nonverbal, nonspeaking, or minimally verbal,* there are two ways that you can modify this exercise. Know that you can do either method depending on what works best at any given time.

    a. First, instead of verbally saying the mantras, say the mantras in your mind while you look at yourself in a mirror or app.

    b. Second, either have your AAC device or another person speak the mantras while you look at your reflection. If you have another person speak the mantras, ask the person to say your name instead of saying the pronoun "I." If you're unsure of which method to try, try both and determine which one feels better to you.

If you would like to tap your collarbone, you can do so regardless of how the sentences are communicated.

Exercise 3: Meditate on surrendering more deeply.

13. *If you would like to meditate with a mantra and need modifications* to engage in meditation, refer to the ACCESS NOTES in the Meditation chapter.

Exercise 4: Read. Read. Read.

14. *If you would like to read the excerpt and reading is challenging for you,* try the following modifications.

    a. Rather than reading the entire excerpt every time, read one paragraph of the excerpt each time you want to read the excerpt.

    b. Alternatively, you can read the following shortened version of the original excerpt every time you want to read it. Please remember that you can change the gender/pronouns in the excerpt below to reflect who you are.

Man is an heir of God and entitled to all that the Father has—all the joy, all the abundance, all the infinity, all the life, all the love, and all the wisdom. Man is entitled to every bit of it, and it is being revealed unto him that his life may be one of Grace and peace.

To each of us will come whatever [brings us joy]. We are so great in God's eyes that he has stored [infinite resources] up for us, that we may know infinite and boundless good.

CHAPTER TWO

prayer

You do not pray to get God to do your bidding. God is not your servant. You pray to have a realization of what God is always doing and being so that your life can bear witness to the Truth, the power, the love, the beauty, the excellence, and the Presence of God.[1]

— REV. MICHAEL BERNARD BECKWITH

I grew up believing that you need to kneel on your knees, fold your hands together, and bow your head in order to pray. When I was a child, I could get into that position pretty easily. Since I was usually crawling around my bedroom floor anyway, crawling over to my bed for prayers was easy peasy. However, by the age of 19, getting on my knees was not so easy peasy. More specifically, getting on my knees was pretty straightforward—after all, that just required a somewhat graceful fall—but now it was the getting up onto my feet that required many prayers, not to mention some help from friends. Once I managed to get off the floor as a 19-year-old, my legs would be in severe pain and spasming quite intensely. Thus, during my first year of college, I had to rethink how I prayed.

By that time, I figured that since God loves us, It could not possibly want us to put ourselves through immense pain and in dangerous situations just to pray. Also, I have friends who are paralyzed from the neck down and cannot kneel. I have other friends who are amputees and do not have knees to kneel on. The Divine is compassionate and all-knowing. Surely, God would not say to my friends who cannot kneel, "I'd love to answer your prayers, but since you have no knees to kneel on, I cannot possibly take the time." No, the God I know is compassionate and says to come simply as you are, so I did. The first time I prayed without kneeling, I did what I could do safely: I bowed my head and folded my hands.

As a child, I held two more beliefs about prayer. First, I thought that if you have a problem, you should pray to God to fix it for you. Second, I believed that if you want something to happen, you should pray that God lets it happen. Thinking back on these moments, I sometimes wonder how I didn't mix God up with Santa Claus. These beliefs about prayer cast God in the role of "fixer" or as an external force that we must beg or beseech in order for It to help us.

But God is everywhere, all around us and within us. So, when we pray "to" God, we are actually aligning our human mind, emotions, and energy with the Divine *within* us so we can be the vessel through which the solution flows. We are praying to unleash the power, majesty, and love of God that resides within us and to channel the energy of those qualities toward a particular situation where our desired outcome *appears* to be missing.

Prayer is a powerful practice that enables us to think differently about our situation. Simply by praying, we are able to expand our consciousness in such a way that our thoughts are no longer consumed by preexisting beliefs, fears, perceptions, and supposed knowledge about the situation. Due to this expansion in our conscious thought, our mind becomes open to intuition, the voice of the Divine.

But how exactly does this happen?

Prayer restores harmony to our subconscious mind and alters any habitual thought patterns found in the conscious mind that are counterproductive to our goal. Additionally, prayer accesses the creative force of the Universe and generates energy that causes our personal energy and the energy of our environment to become in sync with the Divine. Thus, prayer enables us to cease focusing on what we believe about a situation, cease thinking unhelpful thoughts, cease channeling all your energy toward what we are unhappy with, and instead gets us to shift our energy to focus on the Divine. Once we focus on the Divine, we allow God to become increasingly active in our subconscious, which allows us to embody our unity with God. That state of living from our oneness with the Divine is where our desired outcome lies.

Not only does prayer nullify our habitual thoughts. It goes one step further and creates new thought patterns within us that change our perception of the world, and ultimately, our reality. As we pray, we create mental, emotional, and physical energy and focus those energies on the realization of our desire. Simultaneously, the energy of prayer combines with the energy that we generate through the act of praying and enhances the energy that we produce. This tsunami of energy in support of the realization of our dream goes throughout the Universe and causes us to become aligned with our desired outcome, or something similar.

This sounds wonderful, doesn't it? Through the practice of prayer, we can align ourselves with the Divine and then experience what we pray for. However, many people have the experience of praying for something and not receiving what they prayed for, which can be disappointing and may lead some to question the validity of prayer and/or God Itself. To those people, I say: remember, the purpose of prayer is first, and foremost, to embody your unity with the Divine. Once you are living from your connection with God, all blessings and prayed-for desires that are in your highest good will flow to you from that place of unity.

Since the purpose of prayer is to embody our divinity and allow the energy of that embodiment to flow toward the fulfillment of our prayer, praying effectively—i.e., praying so that are our prayers are answered—requires us to pray in such a way that we feel our connection with the Divine. However, we are not always taught how to pray in this manner. Thus, some people feel like praying is akin to rolling dice: sometimes you'll get lucky and have your prayer answered, and sometimes you'll come up short so your prayer won't be answered. But, this would suggest that God's love, goodness, mercy, and abundance are mercurial. The truth of God is that It is always giving, always loving, always generous, and always listening to our desires. So, God is always flowing gifts, blessings, and abundance throughout each of our lives, but we may not be experiencing this goodness, even after we pray.

You may still be wondering why this is. "Isn't it enough to simply pray? After all, I am praying to God. Isn't that feeling my connection to God?" you may be tempted to ask.

Before I continue, I want to emphasize that there is no wrong way to pray. In the same way I realized that prayer didn't have to look a certain way when I was in college, I know that prayer doesn't have to sound a certain way either. Simply praying the words "Help me!" or "Thank you!" is absolutely perfect, sacred, and can be answered. The following suggestions are meant to help you expand your prayer toolkit but are by no means required for a person to pray "appropriately."

That said, praying "to God" is not quite the same as praying to experience and express your oneness with God. Prayers that cause you to feel your connection with God tend to be more effective than praying to God and these prayers contain a few ingredients:

First, authenticity is key to having a prayer answered. God is always giving, *but* It is giving what is for our highest good and what will bring us true happiness. The Divine does not give us what we *think* we want. Thus, praying for something that is not authentic to who you are cannot be answered because receiving that thing would not lead you to true joy.

Second, praying to experience a quality of God is more likely to be answered than praying for a specific item that we think we want. This is because we don't always know what item will bring us what we truly desire. For example, I heard about a teenager who loved painting using acrylic paint. He had been a painter most of his life and was committed to becoming a professional painter.

This young man wanted to enroll in a visual arts program at a prestigious academy near his home. Knowing that this program was highly competitive, his mother told him that he also had to apply to the performing arts program at the academy. The son did not want to do so because he knew he was meant to be a painter; however, his mother insisted that he apply to both programs. The son was so resistant to applying to the performing arts program that his mother asked him why he wanted to apply to the painting program. The boy said he wanted to be fully realized and express what was deep in his soul, and he believed this program would help him do that.

With that information, his mother prayed for him. She didn't pray that he get into a specific program or become a specific type of artist. She prayed that her son would do what would enable him to become fully realized and express what was deep within him. A few weeks later, her son received word that he had been accepted to the performing arts program but rejected from the visual arts program. He was quite upset, of course. Since he had little performing arts experience, a staff member at the school recommended he attend the school's summer performing arts program. The son was less than eager to attend the summer program but did so. He came home after the first day of the summer program with a light in his spirit and a twinkle in his eyes.

When his mother asked him what had changed, he said, "I know why I was rejected from the visual arts program. When I paint, I keep my door and curtains closed in my bedroom, listen to dark music, and sit hunched over. I shut out the world. But when I act onstage, I'm open. Today, I connected with others. I was in the light and expressed happiness in a way I don't when I paint. Mom, I am fully realized when I act."

This is what can happen when you pray to experience a quality of God rather than for a particular thing. By praying for a quality, you give the Universe the flexibility necessary to bring you what you truly want in a way that might be outside your paradigm of how your desire is supposed to manifest.

Third, we must believe that our prayer can be answered. Since God is all-powerful, all-knowing, and is everywhere, God can create anything that is in our highest good. However, we must believe in the infinite nature of God—in Its infinite love, mercy, compassion, power—to realize our prayer, because in order to embody our oneness with God, we must embrace all of God. Embracing all of God means embracing the infinite possibilities of God. If we believe that our prayer is too big to be realized, we are restricting the fullness of God. When we restrict God's fullness, we move out of alignment with God and pray from a sense of limitation and separation from the power and the love of God. When we pray from a sense of separation and limitation, we prevent our prayer from being answered, because any prayer that comes to fruition is realized through our alignment with God. And our alignment with God is, in part, dependent upon our belief in God's infinite creative force.

Fourth, deeply feeling your prayer is another key ingredient of effective prayer. Feeling is emotion, and emotion is energy. The entire Cosmos, God, the Universe, is energy. So when you feel deeply while praying, you are embodying your oneness with the Divine. We were not created to be automatons merely reciting words that mean nothing to us. We were created to feel, to allow energy to move through us, to use energy to create. God used energy to create the Universe. Similarly, when we pray with feeling, we are using energy to create our personal Universe. In this way, we are embodying our Divine nature to use energy as a creative force. When you allow feelings to flow while you pray, you align your energy with the Divine flow. Once you are in that flow, the Divine within you focuses on the area of your life you are praying about. By channeling the love, power, and grace of God in the direction of the content of your prayer, you are allowing the power of God to reveal Itself through the answering of your prayer.

Lastly, releasing your prayer to the Universe is imperative if you want to pray effectively. Releasing your prayer to God means that once you finish your prayer, you release it from your thoughts. After you pray for something you really want, it's tempting to wonder when it will happen, how it will happen, if it will happen, on and on. However, focusing on such thoughts delays the manifestation of your desire because you are focusing on the lack of your desire, which causes you to feel a lack of peace, a lack of happiness, anxiety, and other not-so-great feelings. When you feel less-than-enjoyable feelings, you move yourself out of alignment with the Divine. However, the realization of your desire depends on your alignment with the Divine. As you pray, you move yourself into alignment with the Divine. So, to remain in alignment once you finish your prayer, trust that the prayer is already answered—the wheels are in motion—and release it.

As a college student, I didn't know these ingredients for effective prayer. I simply knew that when I was confronted with an undesirable situation that didn't seem to improve with meditation, it was time to pray like nobody's business!

My freshman year at Scripps College was absolutely fantastic and filled with fun, friends, new experiences, surprising discoveries about myself, and of course, loads of studying. One of the biggest surprises during my first year was that I participated in something called InterVarsity Christian Fellowship (IV for short).

My parents attended church when I was a little girl, which meant I attended church with them. However, as can happen during one's preteen years, around the age of 11 or 12, I told my mom that I didn't want to go to church anymore. Why, you ask? Because it was boring. I may have had a disability, but I was a typical preteen. My mom and I made a deal that I'd go to church, but I'd volunteer in the nursery. I loved playing with babies and toddlers, so this was perfect, for a while.

Once high school came, going to church with my parents was not on my list of top 10 favorite things to do. As a matter of fact, it was nowhere near that list. So, my parents relented and let me stay home on Sunday mornings throughout my high school years. Given my distinct lack of interest in attending church during high school, you can imagine how surprised I was when I found myself voluntarily attending church as a college freshman.

While attending church on campus, I made several friends who attended something called IV. After getting to know each other, they invited me to attend an IV meeting. I had never heard of IV, but hey, I figured I was in college to try new things. I ended up enjoying every minute of it! I got to meet new people who also had a faith life, sing awesome songs, and listen to a perspective on Christianity that differed from what I had grown up with. IV definitely expanded my horizons and my understanding of God. While I didn't resonate with everything that was taught, I appreciated the opportunity to learn and to be in an environment where I could analyze my belief system alongside others.

One of the activities of IV that I absolutely loved was going on retreats. The weekend before the spring semester, I attended IV's winter retreat, which was held at a church off campus. We had a blast at the church, singing songs, studying the Bible, asking our leaders faith-based questions, and just enjoying each other's company. Please understand, we were still typical college-aged young adults. There was plenty of playing around, telling jokes, and being completely inappropriate too. Throughout the entire retreat, I was incredibly grateful for everyone's willingness and openness to help me out whenever necessary. The church wasn't wheelchair accessible, so to go from the main floor to the sleeping quarters, two very strong guys took turns carrying me up and down the steps. I needed help to get ready in the mornings and evenings, and several of the women assisted me with everything I needed. It was a weekend of complete inclusivity and one in which I felt like everyone viewed my needs as simply a part of the weekend—not something I always experienced. It was awesome!

So, when the upper-class students in IV started telling me about the summer retreat, I knew I had to go. The weeklong retreat was scheduled to be held on Catalina Island at the end of the spring semester. In addition to the usual Bible study and worship song sing-alongs, we'd do things like hiking, kayaking, swimming, hanging out on the beach, and meeting Christian Fellowship groups from other colleges. In short, it was camp IV style (and as you will learn in future chapters, I love camp!). I was so excited about the possibility of going, but I was also a bit hesitant.

Our campsite was on the side of a mountain, a developed mountain, but a mountain, nonetheless. In addition to being pretty steep, the campground was covered in sand, grass, and dirt, and just for good measure, large boulders dotted many of the pathways through the camp. As we researched the location, my friends and I quickly realized that the power wheelchair I use for independent mobility on a daily basis was going to have to stay at school, and I'd be rocking my manual wheelchair (chair) for the duration of the retreat. Since I could barely move myself an inch in my manual chair on flat, hardwood floors, going to Catalina Island in my manual wheelchair meant I'd need to rely on my fellow IV members for all my mobility needs in addition to all of my personal care needs for a full seven days.

Questions about the validity of my desire to go on this trip swirled around my head. Was this simply too much to ask of a group of college students? Would they be capable of doing all of this? Do I even know them well enough to trust them this much?

Everyone who knows me will tell you that I am one of the most organized people you'll ever meet. If there's two weeks before a trip and I haven't started packing, something is profoundly wrong! So, naturally, I started packing for Catalina about three weeks before the trip. Although my friends and I hadn't officially discussed my care needs, they were aware I would need help and said that we'd sit down and talk about how everything would work. I said okay, and then we talked about the cool activities we'd do on Catalina. Distracted by the semester coming to a close, I was fine with this at first. After all, everyone had final exams to study for, papers to write, and graduating seniors to say good-bye to. However, once I had finished all of my classwork, the retreat was just a few days away and my friends and I still hadn't had "the talk." Given this turn of events, I became increasingly apprehensive about whether or not I should go on the retreat.

Of course, I really wanted to go, but only if it was in everyone's best interest. I wanted everyone to have a phenomenal time and I wanted everyone to be safe. I simply wasn't sure if those goals were compatible with me going on the retreat.

Then it was suddenly two short days before the trip, and I still hadn't talked to my friends about the logistics. The questions that had been swirling around my head were now screaming in my ear whenever I had a quiet moment. On top of that, additional questions had joined the choir of voices singing quite vociferously in my head: "Are my friends having second thoughts?" "Are they uncomfortable with me going on the retreat, but they don't know how to tell me?" My brain was just chattering on and on. That is, I *thought* my brain chattering on, but in reality, that voice was my ego. Instead of meditating to quiet that voice in my head, I allowed it to continuously "speak" to me, causing me to question my friends.

Further complicating matters was the fact that my dorm was going to be closed during the week of the retreat. So, if I wasn't going on the retreat, I needed to make arrangements for my parents to pick me up. Fortunately, my parents were very patient and also wanted me to have the opportunity to go to Catalina, so they told me to tell them my plans once I knew what I would be doing. However, I really wanted to tell them something as soon as I could.

I was feeling so much anxiety about everything, that I finally just prayed. When I pray in these situations, I pray very informally, and I get out all the emotions I'm experiencing. I remember saying, "God, you know the body you gave me. You know what it can do and what it can't do. I really want to go on this retreat, but only if it's in my friends' and my best interest. If I'm meant to go, then you've got to send some help. If I'm not meant to go, then please show me that. I'm open to whatever is best, but I need you to show me what that is! Thank you, Lord! I love you! Amen!" I prayed with every bit of emotion I had and with such intensity that when I finished, I needed to catch my breath. Within two minutes of ending the prayer, there was a knock on the door.

Still a bit short of breath, I opened the door and, drumroll please, there was one of my friends from IV. Although I was almost certain there were TV cameras in my dorm room, I had to fight the urge to look around and see if I was on the show *Candid Camera*. Instead, I accepted that this was the incredible power of sincere prayer.

My friend came in my room profusely apologizing that someone from our circle of friends hadn't been by sooner. We then sat down, and after chitchatting for a while, she wanted to talk about the retreat. I was fully prepared for her to say that it might be best for me not to go this year, so I took a deep breath and braced myself.

Instead of confirming my fears, my friend explained that when word got out that I wanted to go on the retreat, almost everyone in IV wanted to know what they could do to help me. Given the large number of people who wanted to assist me, my friends created a schedule of volunteers so I'd always have two people ready to help me at any time on the retreat. So many people volunteered to support me on the island that sometimes three or four people were scheduled to assist me.

I simply could not believe what I was hearing. In the span of 30 minutes, my emotions went from high anxiety, to deep prayer, to absolute gratitude and joy. Needless to say, I was certain that the best path for me, and everyone else in IV, was for me to attend the retreat. I was so excited about being able to go, and a bit overwhelmed that so many wanted to make sure I could come along, that my entire body was vibrating.

After the conversation, my friend left and I simply thanked God, not only for the incredible opportunity to go on a retreat with people so committed to full inclusion, but also for answering my prayer so quickly.

Two days passed and it was now time to load into my friend's car for the drive to the ferry that would take us to Catalina Island! I was so excited that I chatted the entire way. Before I knew it, we got off the ferry and were on the island.

The week was one of the best experiences of my life! Every day, I attended classes where my fellow IV members and I studied passages from the Bible, reflected on the meaning of the messages, and talked to others about what we were learning. Between classes, I bonded with the beach, which was absolutely gorgeous. One of the other IV members brought a beach chair, which quickly became known as "Allison's Seat." I loved that beach chair because I could get out of my wheelchair for a while and sit lower to the ground with the rest of the group. I also spent a lot of time kayaking and being on the water.

I met a Black woman from a different college who was also on a retreat with her Christian fellowship. She was legally blind, and we talked any time we could. We both had spent our early childhood years in a Black church, we both had been born with physical disabilities, and we both attended predominantly white colleges. It was awesome to talk to her about my experiences and hear about her experiences, and just hang out.

While I loved just about every minute of the week, one of my favorite experiences came on one of the last evenings of the retreat. Over the course of the retreat, I heard countless people talk about a hike they took on the other side of the island. Apparently, the hike took about

10 minutes, and when you got to the top of the hill, you could see a few other land masses dotting the ocean for miles. It sounded like a beautiful view! And I really wanted to see the view for myself, but hiking with a wheelchair not built for hiking did not seem like a great idea. So, I did the next best thing. I asked a friend to take pictures of the view for me the next time she did the hike.

Joey overheard my request and said, "Allison, do you want to see the view? I could push you up there."

"Yes, I do. But from what I heard, the terrain is pretty steep and rocky and narrow. I'm just not sure how safe it would be for me or you," I replied. By this point, a few people had stopped their conversations and were attentively listening to this conversation.

"Yeah, it is really narrow and kind of slippery," Joey said, sounding a bit reflective, "but I'm sure we could figure something out so you can see the view for yourself. Just say the word and I'll come up with some way to get you up there."

Before I could respond, someone said, "I'll help, and I'm sure Scott will help too."

I smiled and tried to calmly say yes; however, my excitement took over my calmness and I excitedly said, "Let's do this!"

That evening after dinner, a group of us met up at the base of the trail. There were about five men and four women, including me, at the meetup spot.

After a logistical discussion, Joey gently lifted me, Eric and Scott picked up my chair, and we all made our way up the hill. It was exhilarating, exciting, and a bit scary! I felt such an incredible sense of belonging in the group. We were just a group of friends out for an evening hike, and everyone was welcome to join us in whatever way they could—including me. I enjoyed the random conversations that popped up over the course of the hike, checked in with Joey from time to time to see how he was feeling, and simply reveled in participating in a pretty arduous hike.

Once we reached the summit, we all turned to face the ocean. The view was absolutely spectacular! The sun was getting low in the sky. The sky was a beautiful orangey-purple color that was reflected in the water as if we were looking at two skies. The sun's light shimmered in the small waves of the ocean. The shimmering looked like little angels or fireflies were dancing on the water as far as the eye could see.

I simply basked in the beauty of Mother Nature. I wish I could say I thought something profound as I stood with my friends watching the sun set over the Pacific Ocean, but no. I had no profound thought at the time. I was simply a 19-year-old who had successfully completed her freshman year of college and who was hanging out with her friends on a Friday night.

Praying to know the best course outcome for the retreat was crucial for me to be able to attend the summer retreat. Prior to praying for the best outcome, I felt so much fear, worry, and anxiety about the logistics that I had moved myself out of alignment with the flow of God. God is the source of all good things and will naturally bestow all our blessings unto us. However, we must keep ourselves open to receiving the flow of blessings that is ours, and we do this by remaining in joy, peace, gratitude, love, and all the other qualities of the Loving Presence. When I allowed fear, doubt, and worry to become my dominant feelings, I restricted my ability to receive God's goodness. It's okay if this happens. We are human, and sometimes our feelings move us out of alignment with our Highest Selves: God.

But, it is in these moments that we most need to pray. The very act of praying moves us from focusing on feelings of fear or despair to focusing on what we *do* want, which subtly shifts our perspective, thereby shifting our energy. We no longer are solely focused on the hopelessness of a situation of lack or frustration. When we pray, we are shifting our energy into alignment with the Divine, and when we shift our energy, we shift our experience.

Through the act of praying, I released the fear, worry, and anxiety. As I focused on affirming what I knew to be true about God—that It knew the capabilities of my body and the needs of my body to participate in the retreat—I affirmed to myself that God knows me intimately and loves me. This allowed me to release the belief that I was alone in dealing with the situation. By praying for what I truly wanted—for everyone to have a wonderful retreat even if that meant I shouldn't go—and because what I truly wanted was in everyone's best interest, I aligned myself with Divine love and intelligence. By ceasing to focus on whether I should go and whether people wanted to help me, and instead focusing on the action that would serve the greater good for everyone involved, I chose to be of service. And by asking God to show me what was in everyone's best interest, I was allowing myself to be a conduit of God's love for myself and my friends. When you allow yourself to be a conduit of God, you are in full alignment with Its blessings, which means you will receive all of the goodness possible. But, I had to go into prayer to reach that place of alignment.

Some say that you should pray for an answer to your "problem." However, prayer itself is the answer. When we pray, we are aligning ourselves with the Divine, which allows our prayers to be answered. It is not some external deity deciding on a whim to answer our prayer! No, it's our own alignment with the Divine that causes our prayers to be answered.

I grew up with the belief that we pray to God to let things happen. I now understand though, that we actually pray to align ourselves with what we want to happen. God is not an external being or force. God is within us, and when we pray, we are focusing on our connection with the Divine. As we focus on that connection, we are aligning ourselves with our deepest knowing of what is in our, and everyone else's, best interest.

Although some prayers—like the one I prayed about going to Catalina Island—are manifested immediately, we all know what it feels like to pray a prayer that takes so long to be answered that we wonder if our words were sucked into some abyss, never to be heard from again. When this happens, we may be tempted to believe that we are not meant to have that particular prayer answered. However, this is not always the case. Sometimes, we experience a gap in time between praying a prayer and having that prayer manifest so we can prepare ourselves for the manifestation of our prayer. . . a fact I was reminded of recently.

After graduating from MIT with my doctorate, I began working full-time as a professional economist. While I enjoyed the work and had wonderful colleagues, a few weeks after I began working at my dream job, my health began to deteriorate. Initially, I thought everything would resolve itself.

However, this did not happen. Instead, my health became a complete conundrum for me. I did everything I could think of to right this beautiful ship that I call my body. But, regardless of what I tried, this ship kept tilting to the side until it had completely capsized. After trying various traditional treatments for months and getting only momentary relief, I turned to alternative modalities to improve my health. This was when I discovered guided meditation and began studying the chakra system and energy healing. My studies introduced me to a whole new facet of spirituality and spiritual practice that expanded my understanding of God and our place in the Universe. As I continued my studies, I learned about quantum physics and metaphysics.

I became so excited about everything I was learning that I talked about it to whoever seemed remotely interested. And by "remotely interested," I mean whoever was within earshot of my voice and was comfortable with talking about God. I'm pretty sure my family and friends could have written books on these topics based solely on what I told them. As I learned more, I incorporated these new ideas and practices into my spiritual toolkit.

I also began to wonder how metaphysics could be applied to living with a disability. Questions such as, "How can we apply the metaphysical understanding of spirituality to disability?" began to fill my mind. I was so excited by the idea of expanding both the understanding of disability and the application of spiritual principles that I wanted to talk with other disabled people about these ideas.

I knew that I could not be the only person with a disability on planet Earth who was interested in spirituality, energy healing, and the intersection of spirituality and disability. I knew for a fact that if I existed, other like-minded individuals had to exist too. The mission, though, was finding these people. Where exactly do you go when you want to discuss the intersection of quantum physics and the lived experience of disability? That's not exactly run-of-the-mill office cooler conversation. Yet, I knew that there had to be a place where I could talk about these topics with others.

A friend told me about various Christian ministries that speak directly to the experience of disability. While that piqued my interest and was a great starting point, it didn't quite address my current understanding of God. I remember thinking, "I'd love to have a spiritual teacher with a disability who combines the lived experience of disability with spiritual teaching and practices."

What I didn't realize at the time was that I had said a prayer. Sometimes, your prayer can be as simple as a thought of something that you'd love to experience. God is always listening and wants to co-create with you the life of your deepest desires.

About five years after I had this thought, the world as I knew it got turned upside down, inside out, and shaken all about by coronavirus. When initial reports regarding COVID-19 surfaced, I didn't think too much about it. At the time, the virus was in China and sounded fairly innocuous. Of course, I hoped that people would get COVID-19 under control, but I likened it to swine flu, or H1N1, which hadn't impacted my life.

When the governor of my state announced stay-at-home orders, I knew coronavirus was a brand-new frontier for me and for much of the world. My active lifestyle of attending glass-blowing classes, sailing, shopping, going to museums with friends, and participating in other activities came to a sudden halt.

Still, I was a bit dubious about getting too alarmed about this so-called pandemic. So I spoke to my physician, who informed me, in no uncertain terms, that I was at high risk of not doing so well if I contracted the virus and that I needed to take additional steps to keep my body healthy due to the CP. After our chat, it became abundantly clear that I was going to be bonding with my home for quite a while, and only a few people would be allowed to visit me.

This shift in lifestyle was not as massive for me as it was for some. Like many in the disability community, during typical nonpandemic times, I go out at most twice per week due to the physicality of going places. I love meeting people, visiting places, and participating in activities. However, due to my reduced muscle control, every movement I make requires a substantial amount of energy. Researchers have estimated that someone with CP uses three to five times more energy than someone without a disability. So, when I go out once, I have used the same amount of energy that someone without CP uses to go out five times in one day. I'm sure you can extrapolate that I need to rest quite a bit to stay healthy. Thus, spending a lot of time in my home was nothing new for me. What was completely new for me was needing to stay in my apartment for months on end because going outside could threaten my life and feeling like I was playing Russian roulette every time someone came into my home.

In light of this new reality, there was only one thing to do . . . turn my home into an oasis in shades of my favorite color—purple—and fill it with activities that fed my mind, body, and spirit. I began attending classes offered by my church on Zoom. I ordered so many art kits from Amazon that I think Amazon should consider naming a building after me. With the help of my caregivers, I became a master jewelry maker. I read countless books on Audible and was more mindful about connecting with family and friends. Even though there was a pandemic raging outside my home, I was just as busy and engaged as ever.

And then it happened.

One day in late March 2020, I opened my e-mail to see a message from my local rehabilitation hospital, Spaulding Rehabilitation. As I read the e-mail, I became more and more excited. After I let out my third or fourth giggle, my caregiver asked what was happening.

"Spaulding is starting an online sports program! We can sign up for whatever class we want and attend the class LIVE on Zoom!" I said, getting more excited with every word.

I began going to Spaulding during my first year of graduate school at MIT. At that time, I was noticing a slight change in my muscle control, and I figured that having physical therapy and occupational therapy would mitigate the effects of these changes. Since Spaulding is consistently ranked as one of the top five rehabilitation hospitals in America by *U.S. News & World Report,* I was beyond thrilled to learn that I could receive those therapies at Spaulding.

Over the course of my therapies, I learned about Spaulding's summer sports program for disabled adults. Through participating in that program, I learned to windsurf, played wheelchair tennis, kayaked, canoed, and rediscovered my love for cycling. In recent years, Spaulding has expanded its sports programs to be available year-round. In fact, just two weeks before my state went into lockdown, I went rock climbing with Spaulding.

In light of Spaulding's commitment to providing those with disabilities opportunities to live active, healthy, and engaged lifestyles, it was only natural that Spaulding's staff would find a way to offer adults with disabilities opportunities to stay active and connected to a community during the pandemic. Since many with disabilities were at higher risk than the general public of contracting and dying from COVID, we stayed in our homes more than the nondisabled, and thus were even more isolated. So, having opportunities to not only engage in physical activity, but also to socialize with others, was of the utmost importance for our mental and physical health. Spaulding offered multiple adapted sports classes such as chair yoga, weight training, dancing, and aerobic exercise five days per week. Since I love yoga and dancing, I signed up for these classes without a second thought.

Spaulding offered another class that piqued my interest: community drum circle. However, I had never been part of a drum circle, nor did I own a drum. But I loved making music and had taken piano lessons for years as a little one. While playing the piano is more difficult now, I was certain that I could hold a stick and bang something in rhythm with others. The description of the class said that each drum circle would be led by someone named Craig Bautz, who would guide us through sound meditations in addition to teaching us how to drum.

I knew I had to try it out when I read "sound meditation," so I registered for the first class. However, there was one small, itty-bitty question that kept creeping into my otherwise excited mind. What on Earth would be my drum? Fortunately, I had a few days before the first drum circle to answer this question. Over the course of the next couple of days, I experimented making sounds with different items until I hit upon the perfect combination of kitchenware: a wooden spoon and a large silver mixing bowl.

With my bowl and spoon perfectly arranged for maximum sound production whenever I whacked the bowl, I was officially ready for my very first drum circle. I logged into the Zoom meeting, and after a few minutes, about seven screens populated my Zoom window. I was so excited that I danced in my seat.

"Hi, everyone! We're waiting for a few others to join us and then we'll get started," Craig said as faces filled the screen of our Zoom room. After everyone else arrived, Craig introduced himself and asked us each to introduce ourselves and say what we were using as our drum.

After Craig explained his role at Spaulding and his background in leading drum circles, he backed up from his camera to show us that he is a wheelchair user and told us about his disability. I went from being excited about drum circle to being overjoyed. I had no idea that our leader had a disability. My prayer had been answered! With that revelation, I was even more ready to soak up this experience.

"There's a saying among drummers," Craig said. "If you can say it, you can play it. So, I'll come up with a phrase, and I'll beat my drum to the rhythm of the phrase. When you're ready, join in. The phrase is: 'I am drumming, drumming.'"

Craig began to slowly play his drum, saying each word as he pounded out the rhythm on his drum. After Craig played the phrase twice, I joined in. Watching Craig's hands, I cautiously began to play my metal bowl with my wooden spoon. As we continued to play the rhythm, I relaxed, threw caution out the window, and played my "drum" like nobody's business. I was in the pure delight of making music. A metal bowl never sounded so good, if I do say so myself!

However, as much fun as I had drumming that first rhythm, I had no idea that the best part of drumming was just moments away. After a few minutes of drumming this rhythm, Craig yelled "RUMBLE," and then started beating his drum very quickly and loudly.

I, of course, followed suit. Then Craig yelled, "ONE . . . TWO . . . THREE," and hit his drum once very loudly and stopped drumming. All of us participants followed his lead.

I cannot begin to fully express the massive amount of pleasure I got from rumbling on my bowl. There is just something unimaginably cathartic about hitting something as loudly and as quickly as you can. As we rumbled, I could not stop giggling. After we hit our drums as loudly as possible for the last note, I let out a loud, "YEAH!" and started laughing.

Craig and everyone else joined in on my laughter. Craig said, "I think Allison enjoyed that rumble!"

I replied, "I LOVED that rumble!"

With that, I beat my very first phrase on my metal bowl, and I was officially hooked on drum circle. We played another rhythm, and then Craig let us rest our hands.

As we rested, Craig taught us about three different types of drums that he owned. He shared the cultural origin of each drum, the importance of vibrations in our overall health, and the power of drumming to create vibrations that not only shift our own energy, but also shift the energy of the world. He discussed the accessibility of each drum by explaining which drums sit on your lap easily if you are a wheelchair user and which drums are easier to play if you have reduced use of your hands.

His teaching fed my soul as much as playing the drum did, because the teaching spoke to so many parts of me: my love of history, culture, energy healing, and equal access. As I participated in that very first drum circle, I was grateful to be making music, to be engaged in an activity that reflected so much of who I am, and to be taught spiritual principles by a teacher with a disability.

Although I had prayed to have a spiritual teacher with a disability, I didn't realize just how powerful having a disabled teacher would be until the end of our first drum circle. Ten minutes before the conclusion of drum circle,

Craig ended the rhythm we were playing and announced that we would close drum circle with a guided meditation. Since I absolutely love guided meditation, I excitedly put down my wooden spoon, closed my eyes, and listened to his voice. He began the meditation by having us see ourselves on the beach. Craig then instructed us to imagine we were walking on the beach and could feel the sand between our toes. He said, "If you can't walk or cannot feel your toes, use your imagination. In meditation, we can do things with our minds that our bodies may not be able to do outside of meditation." Craig continued, "I'm paralyzed and use a wheelchair, so I haven't walked on a beach or felt sand between my toes in years. But that doesn't matter in meditation. Here, you can create and experience anything you can imagine, and your body receives the same benefits as though you actually had the experience."

In all of the guided meditations I've listened to over my many years of meditating, I never participated in a meditation that spoke so directly to me and my body. The meditation was so powerful that I had to fight back tears. This was the first time that a guided meditation addressed my physical experience of disability and the ability of my meditating mind to create excursions that transcend the physical effects of disability. It was simply awesome!

A few weeks later, Craig focused on the need to be resilient as we navigate the pandemic. Rather than speaking of resiliency in abstract, esoteric terms, he spoke about it within the framework of disability. Since everyone in drum circle has a disability, Craig reminded us that we all have had to be resilient to simply live our lives. He said that if we were born with a disability, we had to be resilient each and every day to learn how to live in a world designed for those with abilities we may not have. And, if we became disabled later in life, we had to be resilient to learn an entirely new way of living our lives.

As he spoke, all of us began nodding our heads in agreement. We all felt empowered and like we could teach the world a thing or two about how to find and seize the gifts that coronavirus was offering us. We carried those feelings of appreciation and pride in our disabilities into our meditation that week.

As our drum circle continued week after week, an awesome thing happened . . . we became a community. Whenever we rested our hands from drumming, we had conversations on various topics. Craig not only allowed these conversations, but he supported and reveled in them as much as we did. During one circle, we spontaneously started talking about our journeys with disability. Everyone who was comfortable participating in the conversation shared amazing things. We found out that two members had had the same surgery when they were infants. They talked about their lives since that operation. Then, one circle member shared that hours after she was born, doctors told her parents she should be institutionalized due to the severity of her disability; however, her parents ignored that advice and decided to care for her at home.

I contributed to the conversation by saying, "My parents were told the same thing about me a few days after I was born. Thank goodness they didn't listen." After discovering that our parents were presented with the same suggestion, we talked about everything we accomplished because our parents decided to raise us at home. Everyone in drum circle shared so much that night. We learned a great deal about each other and our commonalities. It was an incredibly moving evening, and I was reminded of the strength each of us has. Now, please understand that we have as many laughs and hilarious conversations as we do serious conversations in drum circle. One week, one of our circle members revealed that she absolutely loves frogs. She showed us frog drapes, frog pillows, frog napkins, and at least 20 different types of porcelain frogs in her porcelain frog display. I don't think I was alone in thinking, "I didn't even know this much frog-themed home decor existed!" We all enjoyed the tour and asked her different questions about this item or that item. The huge smile on her face conveyed her absolute delight in being our tour guide through frog city.

Two members of our drum circle are a married couple named Agatha and Owen. They have been married for years; both have disabilities and are always a source of hilarious commentary on the events of the day. We can always count on Agatha to tell it like it is. One evening, both Agatha and Owen arrived at drum circle wearing hand splints. Craig, who always keeps an eye on the health of all of the circle members, asked what happened. Agatha explained that she sprained her wrist and Owen had a minor procedure on his hand. Then, she and Owen held each other's hand. As they held hands, they lifted their hands to the sky and Agatha said, "We're the perfect pair. Right now, I can use only my left hand and Owen can only use his right hand, but together we make one perfectly functioning pair of hands!" We all started cracking up laughing at Agatha's blunt but so truthful statement.

I couldn't help but think how that statement perfectly described our drum circle. Yes, we all arrive at circle bringing our unique blend of abilities and, yes, disabilities. And we all fit together perfectly in ways that uplift each other.

Years earlier, when I thought that silent prayer about wanting to have a spiritual teacher with a disability, I had no idea that God would bless me with an incredible teacher and an entire community of people with disabilities, each on their own path of understanding spirituality. However, that's what can happen if you continue to engage in practices that keep you consciously connected with the Divine. God not only blesses you with what you asked for, but It will often expand upon your request and give you even more. Why is that? God loves us, is generous, and is ever-expanding. The Loving Presence wants us to experience joy and evolution while we are on Earth. So, in blessing us with more than we ask for, God not only increases our joy, but It also expands our perspective of what is possible and gives us the opportunity to evolve.

Let's be honest. Sometimes, waiting for a prayer to be answered can be downright hard. About four years after I had expressed my desire for a spiritual teacher with a disability and I still hadn't met one, I thought, "Well, perhaps that's not meant to be." But no! I was meant to have a spiritual teacher with a disability. It just took five years for me to meet him. Why is this? Why do some prayers take so long to be answered? Ernest Holmes offers the following explanation in his book *Prayer,* stating the answer to our prayer

> *is instantly manifest on the invisible plane. "Before they call, will I answer," is the divine promise. . . . [The answer to our prayer] depends solely upon our belief and our acceptance, and our willingness to comply with the Law through which all good comes. . .*
>
> *The Universe will never deny us anything, unless we conceive that it is possible for us to think of something that is impossible for the Universe to produce! Everyone who asks receives, according to his belief.*[2]

Thus, as soon as we pray for a desire that is both authentic and for our greatest good, God has answered that prayer. If we don't experience an immediate manifestation of our desire, we may have some work to do to align ourselves with God and with the belief that our desire is possible for us. Although I prayed to have a spiritual teacher with a disability, I wondered how I would meet the teacher and where the teacher would live. At the time of my prayer, all of the spirituality teachers I followed were located thousands of miles away from me. I had the desire to have a spiritual teacher with a disability, but I did not believe that I would be able to meet with the person easily. So, I had an authentic desire, but I questioned whether my desire could become my reality.

This lack of belief created a misalignment between me and the Divine that delayed the manifestation of my dream. The delay occurred because as Eric Butterworth, a lauded minister, says, "God can only do for you what He can do through you."[3] Which means that even though I prayed to have a spiritual teacher with a disability, I had to be the vessel through which my dream came. I had to take action to allow God to bring a disabled spiritual teacher into my life. What action did I need to take? The action was twofold. First, I needed to cultivate an environment of belief within my mind and soul by continuing to meditate and pray, reading books on spirituality, practicing gratitude, and engaging in spiritual practices.

Once I believed in the possibility of my prayer being answered, the time came for the manifestation of my prayed-for desire, and I flowed into the second action: following the gentle nudges of God that led to my prayer being answered. Since I received Spaulding's e-mail about adaptive sports opportunities after it was clear that I would not be leaving my home due to COVID, I could have said to myself, "I can't leave my home right now, so there's no point in opening this e-mail," and deleted the e-mail. But I didn't. My intuition, which is the voice of the Divine within, told me to open that e-mail. I did and found an abundance of new opportunities that I could enjoy from home. And when that Divine voice spoke to me again and nudged me to sign up for drum circle, I did. Even though at the time, I thought, "I don't have a drum. How is this going to work?" I was still receptive to following the nudge to sign up for drum circle.

At any point along this journey, I could have stopped following those nudges and decided to follow the logical reasoning of my human understanding. However, human understanding is incomplete, so relying solely on human understanding can limit our opportunities. The human brain does not have the infinite intelligence of the Divine. Divine intelligence is limitless. Thus, when we remain aligned with the Divine, we remain aligned with infinite intelligence, which knows how and when to answer our prayers in the way that is most perfect for us.

HOW TO PRAY

Exercises and Prompts

While there are many forms of prayer, one of the most effective types of prayer is affirmative prayer. Affirmative prayer is so effective because "it reflects the certainty that we are each being led to our highest good, despite any temporary appearances."[4] It involves praying in such a way that you feel as though you already have the essence of what you are praying for. For example, if you're praying for a new car, affirmative prayer enables you to feel at this moment how you feel when you have a safe, reliable, affordable, and easy means of transportation. When you pray an affirmative prayer, you focus on already having the essence of your desire rather than focusing on wanting the object of your desire. For example, in a non-affirmative prayer, one might say: "Please God, help me find a house." In contrast, an affirmative prayer might be: "I am now guided to my perfect home." Affirmative prayer allows us to practice having the feeling of what we seek before we attain our desire.

The exercises in this section are divided into two categories based on your comfort level with affirmative prayer: exercises for those who are completely new to affirmative prayer and exercises for those who are ready to write their own affirmative prayer.

If you're new to praying affirmative prayer and unsure of how to pray "correctly," try the following exercise.

Exercise 1: Read affirmative prayers.

I recommend reading the affirmative prayers contained in one of the following two books. Each book is organized by topic. For example, if you would like to pray a prayer about improving your health, you'd turn to the page with that prayer.

1. *Prayer: How to Pray Effectively from the Science of Mind* by Ernest Holmes
2. *Get Over It! Thought Therapy for Healing the Hard Stuff* by Iyanla Vanzant

If you are ready to take the leap and pray your own affirmative prayer, this exercise is just for you.

Exercise 2: Write and pray your own affirmative prayer.

a. *Prepare to write your affirmative prayer.* I list the five steps of an affirmative prayer under section b. of this exercise. However, before you dive into the five steps, do the following:

   i. *Write down what you are praying about.* Are you praying about relationships, finances, family, career, etc.? Whatever it is, write down the precise situation.

   ii. *Consult page 18 and the list of qualities of God.* Determine which of these qualities you believe are missing from the situation. For example, if the situation is you want a job you like that pays better, then you might select joyful abundance as the quality for your prayer.

   iii. *Write down the quality (or qualities) you selected.*

b. *Write down at least one sentence for each step of your affirmative prayer.* Although many churches have their own version, this particular five-step affirmative prayer was written by Howard Voyles at the Creative Living Foundation:

   Step 1 – Recognition: Recognize that God is present in, around, and through all things and that God is the source of all. A sample sentence is, "I recognize that God is everywhere, present at all times, and all things emanate from the Divine."

Step 2 – Unification: Acknowledge that we are all connected and interdependent. We are all one, and we are all one with the Divine. Two sample sentences are, "Since God is everywhere always, God is right here in me, and this is true for everyone. So we are all one because we are all one with God."

Step 3 – Realization: Realize that because we are one with the Divine, that which is for our highest good is already one with us. Insert the quality or qualities from *Exercise 2a* into this step. A sample sentence is, "Since I'm one with God, I know that joyful abundance is right here, right now, in every moment of my life because I am joyful abundance!"

Step 4 – Thanksgiving: Express gratitude for the manifestation of what you have prayed for. Know that you have aligned yourself with your desire. Deeply feel appreciation as you say this part of your prayer. This is one of the most important steps in affirmative prayer. Two sample sentences are, "I am so incredibly grateful, God, to experience joyful abundance right now! Thank you, thank you, thank you!"

Step 5 – Release: Release your prayer to the Divine and trust that it is done. Three sample sentences are (you can say any one of these, or all of them), "I release this prayer to the Universe. And so it is! Amen."

c. Now it's time to pray. With your newly written affirmative prayer in hand, there's just one thing left to do . . . pray! That's right. Read your affirmative prayer out loud with all of the emotion and energy you can muster.

ACCESS NOTES

Exercise 2: Write and pray your own affirmative prayer.

1. *If you have Attention Deficit Hyperactivity Disorder (ADHD) or difficulty focusing while praying*, the following suggestions may make praying more accessible to you.[5]

    a. If writing out entire sentences is not possible, try writing out a bullet-point list for each step in your affirmative prayer.

    b. Pray in a quiet place in your home. If possible, designate this as your prayer space and don't do anything else in this space. Also, hang a picture that symbolizes spirituality to you in this space.

    c. Before you begin praying, take a few deep breaths to relax your body.

    d. If your hands or body get fidgety, manipulate a stim/fidget device while you pray. God does not care what you are doing with your hands when you pray as long as you are feeling your prayer as deeply as possible.

    e. If sitting still while praying is too difficult, try praying while exercising.

2. *If you are nonverbal, nonspeaking, or minimally verbal, and want to pray,* I suggest doing the following experiment to determine how

to make your prayer practice as effective as possible:

a. First, if use an AAC device with the capability to speak what you type into it, type the prayer into your device. Have your AAC device speak the prayer. As your device is saying the prayer, feel as much passion and emotion as possible.

b. Second, ask someone to read your prayer out loud as you listen.

c. Third, say the prayer in your head with as much passion and emotion as you can.

d. Once you finish, determine which method enabled you to feel your prayer the most deeply. Speaking your prayer is not required to pray effectively; however, deeply feeling the words of your prayer is required for it to be effective. Select the method of praying (either saying the prayer in your head, having your AAC device speak your prayer, or having someone else speak your prayer) that allows you to most deeply feel your prayer.

3. *If typing or writing is a tiring or time-consuming process,* try the following ways of composing your prayer to determine which one is the best for you:

a. Write or type a bullet-point list for each step in the affirmative prayer.

b. Write or type full sentences (or bullet-point lists) for each step over the course of two or three days. You don't have to write your entire prayer at once.

4. *If you need a simplified version of an affirmative prayer that you can pray for any situation,* read the following prayer out loud with as much feeling as possible. If you cannot read, or if you can't speak, you can have someone read the prayer to you, and you can repeat the words you are able to say. Or someone can read the prayer to you while you close your eyes and deeply feel the prayer.

God is everywhere all the time. I am one with the Divine. I know that love, intelligence, and right action are the only things I experience, because I am one with the One! Thank you, thank you, thank you for the perfect manifestation of this prayer! And so it is! Amen.

CHAPTER THREE

grace

Grace is the natural state of every Son of God.[1]

— *A COURSE IN MIRACLES*

Growing up, I sang my share of hymns in church. One of the hymns that I remember singing no matter what church I was attending or what denomination the church happened to be was "Amazing Grace." When I was a child and a teenager, the song was ubiquitous. Almost everywhere I went, "Amazing Grace" seemed to be waiting for my arrival. I was always struck by just how many churches sang the song and how often I saw the song performed on various television shows.

I didn't even need to go to church or turn on the television to get my seemingly monthly dose of the song, because my sister was on the "Amazing Grace" bandwagon too. My sister loved that song so much that she sang it around the house as she went about her daily routine. I remember this vividly because she also loved up-tempo songs with very risqué lyrics, so the contrast between the songs that would usually blast from the radio in her room, and her singing the slow, sedate, G-rated "Amazing Grace" would always make me crack up laughing.

Although I was surrounded by "Amazing Grace," other than knowing that grace was a sweet sound that saved "wretches" (as the hymn says), I had no concrete idea of what grace was exactly. The fact that everyone on the planet, or so it seemed, innately understood how *amazing* grace was piqued my interest. I wanted to be a part of the "I understand grace and absolutely love it" club too! However, by the end of high school, I was still trying to figure out what grace was and how it applied to me. As a college student, I decided to go on a quest to once and for all unearth the beauty of grace.

I began this quest by looking for references to grace in the Bible in the hopes of understanding it better. You should understand that as a college student, there was exactly one time per week that I'd actually read my Bible. I'm pretty sure you know when that one time per week was: in church. Outside of church, I rarely just picked up my Bible and read it. So, my decision to choose to read the Bible on my own meant that I was serious about figuring out the answer to this question. Unfortunately, my Bible reading did not help me in my quest to understand grace.

A few months after my less-than-successful attempt, I watched one of my favorite television shows at the time: *Starting Over.* One of the show's co-hosts, minister and best-selling author Iyanla Vanzant, was working with a client who needed to learn about grace. Mrs. Vanzant illustrated one form grace can take by having her client complete an exercise. By the end of the episode, I understood that grace is a gift from God. Grace is an act of God that helps us in any endeavor that is in our best interest. Mrs. Vanzant demonstrated that grace is the energy that coordinates supportive experiences and situations that aid us in realizing those goals that we cannot achieve by ourselves despite our best efforts. At the moment it looks like we are not going to reach our goal, something or someone comes along completely unexpectedly and helps us make it a reality. These occurrences are demonstrations of God's grace. I mulled this definition over in my mind for weeks after watching the show, trying to gain even more insight into grace. Now that I had a partial understanding of the word, I wanted to go further. I wanted a complete and holistic understanding of grace.

A few months later, my desire to gain a complete understanding of grace was answered a little more when I heard about a newly released book called *The Unmistakable Touch of Grace*. Of course, I bought the book and read it cover to cover. I knew I had been guided to the perfect resource to learn even more about grace when I read page two of the book, where Cheryl Richardson writes,

> *Grace comes from the Latin gratia, meaning favor, charm, or thanks. Spiritual traditions from around the world each share a similar understanding of this word. . . . In Christian terms, grace is defined as the infinite love, mercy, favor, and goodwill shown by God to humankind. In Judaism, the concept of grace is expressed by the Hebrew word hesed, meaning mercy, or loving-kindness. Grace is seen as a creative force—an act of exceptional kindness and goodness.*[2]

After studying grace so thoroughly, I can often spot it from a mile away. Although I spent many—and I do mean *many*—days taking final exams, one of these stands out as the most grace-filled exam day of my life. Not so much because of what happened during the exam, but because of the events that followed.

During the fall semester of my fourth year of graduate school at MIT, I took development economics. In the days leading up to my final exam, local meteorologists forecasted a light snowfall would begin a few hours after my exam ended. The snow would amount to about one or two inches. Since it was December in Massachusetts, a light snowfall was nothing of note. I love watching snow as it falls, so I was excited by the prospect of having a picturesque snowfall to look forward to after taking my final exam.

The morning of my exam, I got in line to board MIT's shuttle bus. Once the bus driver, Kent, saw me, he deployed the ramp so I could get on the bus.

"You're up and at 'em early today, Allison," Kent said as he secured my wheelchair to the floor of the bus.

"Yeah! I have a 10 A.M. final," I replied as I settled in for the 15-minute bus ride from my dorm to the economics building. When we arrived, Kent wished me luck, and before I knew it, my clock read 10:00 A.M. and my scribe arrived with my exam in hand. We exchanged a few pleasantries and then it was time to bust a move . . . exam style.

Three hours later, with my exam complete, I bundled up to catch the shuttle back to my dorm. After locking my office door, I drove my power wheelchair (chair) down a windowless hallway and pressed the button to open the automatic doors that led to a hallway with floor-to-ceiling windows. As soon as I got to the first window, I stopped dead in my tracks.

The light snowfall that was supposed to start after my exam ended had already started. And it wasn't a "light snowfall." It was a bona fide blizzard!

"How could I tell that we were in the midst of a blizzard?" you might ask.

Well, normally, you could see the Charles River and the entire Boston skyline through those windows. On this day, however, the snow was coming down so hard that all you could see was a wall of white. You couldn't even see individual snowflakes. It looked like someone had draped a white sheet over the window.

After taking in this sight for a moment and not completely believing what my eyes were seeing, I cranked the speed dial on my wheelchair's controller as high as it could go and drove my chair at top speed back to my office. Mario Andretti had nothing on me that day! I'm pretty sure I left a few skid marks on the floor as I raced back to my office. Once in my office, I logged into my computer and opened the Internet browser to MIT's homepage only to have my worst fear confirmed.

In bold, large letters read the following words: "EFFECTIVE AT NOON, MIT IS CLOSED. ALL OFFICES ARE CLOSED." It was currently a little after 1:00 P.M. This meant that MIT's transportation department, which ran the shuttle that I depended on to get around campus, was closed and there was no shuttle service!

Why was this a big deal? During my first summer at MIT, I decided to drive my power wheelchair from my dorm to the economics building. About 10 minutes into the jaunt, I realized that I had made an error in judgment. The sidewalks were so bumpy and at such steep angles that my chair almost tipped over a few times. To prevent my chair from tipping over every time I rolled over a steep angle, I leaned forward with all my might to counteract the force pulling my chair backward or sideways. Whenever I drove over a bump, a jarring sensation would travel up my back and down my legs, causing my muscles to tighten and then spasm. As I drove over more bumps, each spasm became more intense and lasted longer. Some sidewalks lacked curb cuts, which meant I had to drive my chair in the street for part of the way.

The trip involved almost an hour of driving my chair over such difficult terrain that by the time I got to the economics building, my muscles were hurting as though I had just run the Boston Marathon and were spasming uncontrollably. And this excursion was on a sunny, warm day with no precipitation. Based on that experience, I knew that driving my chair over the same terrain in a blizzard would be downright dangerous, if not impossible.

Although my mind kept saying, "Can I panic now? Please let me panic now! Isn't this the perfect time to panic?" I knew that there was a solution to this situation that didn't involve me sleeping in my office or driving my chair through a blizzard. The disciplined attitude that my daily spiritual practice cultivated in me came shining forth. When my mind wanted to go into panic mode, I refused to let it. Because I consciously refused to panic, my spirit was able to speak to me. That quote from the Bible came to my awareness: "Be still and know that I am God." In an instant, I knew I needed to be still by quieting my mind.

Even though the situation appeared to be that I was stranded in a classroom building an hour away from my home with no one to help me get there, the truth of the situation was that God was right there with me, in me and around me. Because God was with me, I was not alone in handling this, and the solution to this situation was right there. I just had to sit quietly and trust myself to find it. I had to embody my oneness with the

Divine by expanding my consciousness beyond the worry of this seemingly impossible set of circumstances into the consciousness of the Divine, where grace flows freely and unceasingly. Consciousness has more than one meaning, but metaphysics teaches that consciousness

> *is the sense of awareness. . . . The knowledge or realization of any idea, object, or condition. The sum total of all ideas accumulated in and affecting man's present being. The composite of ideas, thoughts, emotions, sensation, and knowledge that makes up the conscious, subconscious, and superconscious phases of mind. It includes all that man is aware of—spirit, soul, and body.*[3]

Had I panicked, I would have experienced the results of being in sense or material consciousness, which is "a mental state formed from believing in and acting through the senses."[4] Sense, or material, consciousness leads to a very constricted way of experiencing the world, because this state of mind rests upon the belief that things are always as they appear, and since the Divine is not observable by the senses, it is not present. When you behave from this consciousness, you believe that the only objects that exist are those that you can see, touch, hear, smell, or taste—depending on your physical abilities. Because humans are so sense oriented, we can move ourselves out of alignment with the Divine—or the realm of the nonphysical—and cut ourselves off from the flow of grace. I had to choose to expand my consciousness beyond sense consciousness and into Divine consciousness.

When we're experiencing a challenging time, it's very easy and quite tempting to become myopic—that is, to focus exclusively on the untenable nature of the undesirable situation, think of every single worst-case scenario, and lament about how bad the situation is. However, when we focus exclusively on that, we constrict our consciousness to sense consciousness, which causes us to be aware of, and open to, only a tiny sliver of the brilliance, beauty, and love of the Divine. From such a consciousness, we cut ourselves off from the grace—the giving nature of the Divine—that is always flowing. We don't need to earn grace, for grace is a gift from God that is always flowing to each and every one of us.

However—and this is a crucial "however"—we must be receptive to the grace that is always available to us. We cannot experience grace if we do not open ourselves up to receive grace. The way to open yourself up to receive grace is to expand your consciousness to Divine consciousness. In the state of expanded consciousness, you are able to receive what is always enveloping you: the generous and constant presence of the Divine.

Thus, as I sat quietly, trying to determine my next step, I consciously chose to focus on the spiritual truth that there was a solution for this situation. By choosing to focus on the existence of a solution, I caused my consciousness to expand until I became receptive to the grace that was surrounding me. And, *eureka*—I received a memory. Not just any memory. A memory that held the key for me to unlock and experience the grace that encompassed me that day. Through God's grace, I remembered a meeting I had with the operations manager of MIT Parking and Transportation, Adam, and the director of MIT's Office of Disability and Access Services to discuss my transportation needs. Since the meeting took place during my first year at MIT, I hadn't thought about it in a few years.

However, on this day, once I had expanded my consciousness enough, I remembered that at the end of the meeting, Adam programmed his phone number into my cellphone. He told me to call him if I ever had an emergency. I considered my current situation for a millisecond and determined that yes, this indeed was an emergency. So, I whipped out my cellphone and called him as quickly as my fingers would move.

"Hi, Adam. This is Allison Thompkins," I said, trying to stay calm.

"Oh yes. Hi Allison."

"I'm calling because I just finished taking an exam in the economics building, and I just read that all of MIT's offices are closed. Is there any way someone can help me get back home?"

"We've been waiting for your call. Kent stayed in the transportation office so he could bring you home. I'll let him know you're ready. The roads are bad, so it'll take him an hour or so to get to you. Sit tight. We're going to get you home, okay?"

I breathed the loudest sigh of relief in my life. "Sounds great! Thank you."

After we hung up, I stayed in my office for a while and then made my way down to the lobby of the economics building, where I waited for Kent. Approximately 30 minutes after I got to the lobby, MIT's shuttle bus slowly pulled up to the economics building. After the bus came to a full stop, I ventured out of the building and, very slowly, made my way to the bus.

Once I was on board, Kent quickly closed the door, turned on the heat, and began securing my chair to the floor of the bus.

"How did you know I was still here?" I asked.

He smiled and said, "I knew I dropped you off for your exam, but I hadn't driven you home yet."

"Thank you for waiting for me."

"You know we're going to make sure you're okay, Allison. Now, these roads are really bad. So it's going to be a good two hours before I can get you home."

"That's okay! As long as I have a safe way to get home and heat, I'm great!"

Kent laughed as we joined the line of cars turning onto the main road. Although Adam had told me that Kent would drive me home, I didn't begin to relax until I was on the bus and we were driving toward my dorm. Once we were on the road, I closed my eyes and took a few deep, calming breaths to ease my body and my mind. This was the first time since I began my exam some four-and-a-half hours earlier that I allowed myself to relax.

Now that I was on my way home, I turned my attention to my next task: letting my caregiver know that she had the night off. Every evening, I had a caregiver come by to help with dinner, general household chores, and getting ready for bed. However, the conditions were so bad, and getting worse by the second, that it wasn't safe for her to come into work.

So, I called her.

"Hi, Amber. This is Allison. I'm calling to let you know that you don't have to come in tonight. The roads are really bad," I said as the bus slowly moved over the snowy roads and around other cars that had stalled or spun out.

"Hi Allison! Oh. I've been on the road coming to your place for the past 30 minutes. Do you not want me to come tonight? How are you gonna get your dinner?"

"Oh no! I want you to come! I just didn't want you to be in any danger. Honestly, I was just going to skip dinner tonight. But, as long as you feel safe out here, I could definitely use the help."

"Yeah, it's fine. I've just got to drive slow. I planned to come in because I know how tired you get after taking exams. I didn't want anything happening to you because you were tired, and I wasn't there to help you."

"Okay. Thank you! Just be careful."

"I will. I might be a little late, but I'll be there as soon as I can."

"That's totally fine! I'll see you soon. Well, soonish."

Amber giggled as she said, "I'll see you soonish, Allison."

After nearly two hours on the road, watching the light of day turn into the darkness of early evening and sharing some laughs with Kent, we finally pulled up to the front of my dormitory.

"Sit tight. I'm going to clear a path for you to get to the front door," Kent said as he prepared to go outside.

As he started clearing a path for me, the dorm manager came out with a shovel to help Kent. Once the two were satisfied with the pathway, Kent came back on the bus and began to untie my wheelchair from the floor of the bus. I couldn't thank him enough for his kindness in that moment.

I drove down the hallway to my dorm room, swiped my identification card, and found myself just sitting in my kitchen, a little overwhelmed. I closed my eyes and thanked God for the grace that enveloped me throughout the day. Although the afternoon was in no way, shape, or form what I planned on, I knew I was held in God's grace nonetheless.

Grace is often extended to us through the loving and kind deeds of others. That snowy afternoon, Adam, Kent, and Amber chose to be instruments of God's grace. But, for me to experience the grace extended to me through the people in my life, I had to do my part. First, I had to expand my consciousness so that I was in alignment with love—I had to look past the dire facts of the situation and the panic to see the truth of God's presence. Once I was in alignment, I became aware of the grace that was continuously flowing into my life.

Second, to actually experience the grace that was flowing all around me, I had to be receptive to grace. If I had expanded my consciousness enough to remember my meeting with Adam, but I said to myself, "I'm not going to call him because he might not answer the phone. Or he might not remember me, or he might not be willing to help me," I would have been unreceptive to the grace that was trying to get me home safely. So, to experience grace, you need to expand your consciousness so that you are aligned with the Divine and be receptive to receiving grace.

Since being in a state of expanded consciousness is a key part of experiencing grace, you may ask, "How in the world do I calm down enough to expand my consciousness when I'm stressed out or fearful about a situation?" Fair question. The answer is you routinely practice being in that state during relatively stress-free, peaceful times in your life through regularly engaging in spiritual activities. Keeping your consciousness expanded, or remembering to expand your consciousness, in the midst of a challenging circumstance is easier when you engage in spiritual practice on a regular basis. It's like creating a spiritual muscle memory that gets stronger and more natural each time you use it.

When you have a regular spiritual practice, you spend more time embodying your oneness with the Divine, expanding your consciousness to Divine consciousness, and soaking in the realm of the nonphysical during relaxing, stress-free times. By regularly and consciously connecting with the Divine, you manifest a spiritual discipline, a habit if you will, that makes you more likely to access this skill during challenging times. In essence, expanding your consciousness becomes your default mode, so when stressful situations arise, you almost automatically seek to expand your consciousness. In this way, having a regular spiritual practice causes you to experience grace more readily than those without such a practice.

Now, please note that in those first anxious moments as I sat in my office at MIT, I didn't know what the solution was. I didn't focus on exactly how I would get home during the blizzard. I simply focused on the fact that there was a solution that was perfect for me. We don't have to know how grace should show up in order to experience its powerful effects. We only need to focus on God's love for us, on the fact that there is a solution to all things, and on being open to receiving that solution. That is enough to expand your consciousness.

At so many points throughout that day, God's grace was poured on me. From remembering Adam's offer, to Kent staying at MIT to make sure that I got home safely, to Amber insisting on coming to help me despite the inclement weather, grace was present whenever I needed it. Every time I needed help, something or someone unexpectedly stepped in to assist me. Receiving assistance whenever you need help is one of the benefits of living in a state of grace, which is "living in a disciplined awareness of the Divine flow."[5]

To consistently experience God's influence in your life and to know on a deep level that everything will work out in the end is to live in a state of grace. It's not something you can demand or beg for from God, but it's a natural result of aligning yourself with the flow of the Divine. And as we know, that level of conscious connection with God comes only through commitment to a spiritual practice, such as meditation, prayer, study, forgiveness, or authentic service to others.

People can experience grace even without engaging in spiritual practice, because God loves each of us and wants the best for us. But, those without a spiritual practice aren't able to live in a constant state of grace. The grace they experience is unpredictable, fleeting, and occurs less often than with those who consistently engage in spiritual practices. This is because those without a spiritual practice are not remaining aligned with God. The grace of God resides in the flow of God. If we want to live in a state of grace, we must remain in the flow of God, which requires diligence and consistent dedication.

Furthermore, since God's grace is often extended to us through the loving, kindhearted deeds of other human beings, we can be conduits of God's grace by extending love, understanding, and kindness to others. When we allow ourselves to be used as instruments of God's grace, we are not only fulfilling our role in the unfolding of God's Divine plan for the world, but we are aligning ourselves with the Divine by allowing God's love, mercy, and goodwill to flow through us. This, in turn, ushers more grace into our lives in two ways. First, when we give grace, we receive grace, because metaphysics teaches that we are all one spiritually, so whatever you do for or give to another person, you are doing for and giving to yourself. Second, when we are conduits of grace, we expand our awareness of our oneness with the Divine, which expands our capacity to receive. Thus, grace is not only a gift that each and every person can receive because God loves us, but grace is also an energy we can circulate by performing acts of kindness for others.

HOW TO LIVE IN GRACE

Exercises and Prompts

Since grace is something we receive *and* something we extend to others, this section offers suggestions on how to receive more (because you already are receiving it) and how to be a conduit of grace.

Exercise 1: Focus on your spiritual practice.

Whether you meditate, pray, attend church services, or do some other personal ritual of connection, these acts bring you closer to God. Since grace is a gift from God, to experience more grace than you already do, you will need to spend more time in communion with the Divine. This will increase your openness to, and receptivity of, the energy of the Divine. Your increased receptivity to the flow of God will increase the amount of grace you experience.

Exercise 2: Express gratitude on the page by keeping a journal.

Write down all of the grace-filled experiences you have each day. I recommend writing in this journal daily, if possible. If this is not possible, write in it as frequently as you can. You may be wondering, "What is a 'grace-filled experience'?" A grace-filled experience can be as simple as a stranger smiling at you or holding a door open for you or someone complimenting you. Grace is any act of unexpected kindness and love you experience. Journaling about the grace you experience will help you see just how much grace you already have in your life *and* will usher even more grace into your life because you will be focusing your mind on grace, and whatever you focus on increases in your life.

If you want to increase the power of your grace journaling, express gratitude for each experience you write down in your journal. After you have finished writing the grace you experienced that day, set a timer for between 5 and 10 minutes and say how grateful you are for each expression of grace you experienced. When doing this exercise, *feel* grateful at the deepest level of your being. Expressing and feeling gratitude for something brings more experiences of that something into your life. See my Gratitude chapter for a discussion of this.

Exercise 3: Become a conduit.

Do acts of kindness and love for the people in your life. From the metaphysical understanding of spirituality, we are all one. Thus, as you perform acts of grace for other people, you are actually receiving grace yourself. Acts of grace can include sweeping a neighbor's porch, buying a cup of coffee for a colleague, smiling at a neighbor, or sending a note with a kind message to a family member or friend. For further discussion of how being kind to others is a spiritual practice, read the chapter entitled Service.

Exercise 4: Express gratitude in the moment.

To amp up the spiritual juice of the acts of grace you perform, express gratitude for being able to perform each act. You can express your gratitude verbally or silently after each act. You just want to *feel* the gratitude as you give thanks for each action. Expressing gratitude for the grace you perform will give you more opportunities to extend God's grace to others. As you perform more acts of grace, you will not only expand the types of grace you bestow on others, but you will also expand the types of grace you *receive*.

ACCESS NOTES

Exercise 2: Express gratitude on the page by keeping a journal.

1. *If writing/typing in a journal on a daily basis is not possible,* try the following modifications.

    a. Write in your journal on a weekly or biweekly schedule.

    b. Either say, sign, or make a mental list of all of the acts of grace you received on a daily or weekly basis. If you're interested in verbal, sign, or mental journaling, I suggest keeping your eyes closed so that you can maintain your focus.

Exercise 3: Become a conduit.

2. *For some in the disability community, leaving our homes or our beds can be challenging or not possible.* If this is the case for you and you still want to be a conduit of God's grace, please read my ACCESS NOTES in the Service chapter for suggestions of acts that can be performed from home or from bed.

CHAPTER FOUR

synchronicity

We do not create our destiny; we participate in its unfolding. Synchronicity works as a catalyst toward the working out of that destiny.[1]

— DAVID RICHO

When I first learned about the concept of synchronicity from my mother, I thought of it as God ordering events of our lives like a tour guide, so we experience the greatest joy in the easiest way possible. I imagined God giggling as humans happened upon Its plan and were left marveling at the sometimes unfathomable and seemingly magical unfolding of our desires.

It would be a few years before I learned that Carl Jung, a 20th century psychologist, created the word to describe "circumstances that appear meaningfully related yet lack a causal connection."[2] According to Jung, life is not simply a series of random events, but rather is an expression of a deeper order, which he named *unus mundus*, and every human being is connected to every other human being. The purpose of synchronicity to Jung was to nudge human beings to shift their conscious thinking to connect to the greater "universal awareness"—which is another name for God, or the Divine. Jung believed that a person could experience a spiritual awakening simply by becoming aware of the synchronicity in their life.

Spiritual teachers and metaphysicians teach us that synchronicity is the careful orchestration of events by the Divine to let us know that we are on the correct path and to help us along that path. Synchronicity is a string of events that have meaning to you but cannot be explained by cause and effect. But what does that mean on a practical level? What constitutes a synchronicity? A synchronicity can take many forms, depending on the individual and the circumstance. For example, seeing the same sequence of numbers repeatedly, hearing a name or phrase that is meaningful to you again and again, or thinking about a desire and then experiencing that desire immediately after. While synchronicity can be a singular occurrence, often it unfolds as a series of signs and coincidences that lead to a joyful, unexpected outcome. Sometimes, the outcome is something we never could have imagined would bring us joy.

In light of the chapter on Grace and the definition of synchronicity, some may be wondering, "What is the difference between grace and synchronicity?" Great question. You can think of grace and synchronicity like you would think of the words *vehicle* and *minivan*. A minivan is one type of vehicle; they are not separate entities. The word *vehicle* refers to many items, and a minivan is one of those items. The same is true for grace and synchronicity. Grace comes in many forms. Synchronicity is simply one form of grace. At this point you may be thinking, "Allison, synchronicity sounds awesome, and I definitely want to have it in my life, but is synchronicity really a spiritual practice? I mean, can you go somewhere and 'synchronicity' like you can go somewhere and pray or meditate?" To which I say: you are right. You can't exactly synchronicity like you can pray, *but* as you recognize patterns and moments of serendipity for what they are and follow the path laid out before you like a trail of breadcrumbs through the forest, you are in the flow of the Divine, expanding your awareness of God and embodying your oneness with the Universe. Recognizing these moments of synchronicity enables you to live from your unity with God, and that conscious choice, that raised awareness, is a spiritual practice.

When you experience circumstances that bring you joy and recognize that those circumstances are created by God, you are affirming the presence and the power of God. This means you are choosing to expand your awareness to better understand God and to realize Its impact on your life on a deeper level. As you expand your awareness and deepen your understanding of God's presence in your life, you are engaging in a spiritual practice and ushering more synchronicity into your life. Spiritual practice helps us become increasingly aware of, and increasingly embody, God's love for us. As you recognize synchronicities for what they are—i.e., demonstrations of God's love, power, intelligence, and grace toward each of us—you are affirming and embodying the presence and the power of God in all things. For me, synchronicity led me to a field of study I never knew I was created to love.

God has given each of us a unique blend of gifts, talents, abilities, and passions, and wants us to express our unique blend in a way that brings joy to us and uplifts the world. Synchronicity is one way that God shows us how to express our unique blend for our personal joy and for the greater unfolding of the world. However, as Aletheia

Luna writes, "Synchronicity seems to be experienced most commonly by those who choose to walk the inner path of self-transformation and enlightenment."[3] In other words, synchronicity is experienced more frequently by those who engage in spiritual practices, because they are the ones paying attention, looking out for messages, waiting for answers to prayers, and embodying their oneness with the Divine. Since God knows exactly what will bring each of us our greatest joy, there is a plan or blueprint of how God would like things to unfold. As Marianne Williamson, respected teacher of *A Course in Miracles*, says, "Every acorn is already programmed to become an oak tree, every embryo is programmed to become a baby."[4]

However, unlike an embryo or an acorn, human adults have a choice of whether we choose to go with the flow of the Divine—to surrender—or to go against it. When we engage in spiritual practices, we are more likely to flow with the loving energy of the Divine and to take action that is in alignment with God's plan. As a result, we experience synchronicity because God does everything It can to support us in fulfilling Its Divine plan. The Divine is intentional. My commitment to spiritual practices led me on a journey of synchronicity that revealed my affinity for development economics.

The summer before I began my Ph.D. studies at MIT, I lived on the campus of George Washington University in Washington, DC. Although I had spent many one-week vacations there, I absolutely loved spending an entire summer in DC because I was able to immerse myself in the culture of the city in a way I never had before. During the week, I worked at my internship at the U.S. Equal Employment Opportunity Commission and on the weekends, I explored the city.

And when I say that I "explored the city," I really mean it. Combine the fact that Washington, DC, is one of the most accessible cities in America—wheelchair users can get to most places in the city completely independently—with the fact that I had a motorized wheelchair (chair) with the second-largest battery available to power chair users, meaning I could drive my chair for miles on a single charge, and you will get an Allison who visited every nook and cranny of DC. I went to so many places that toward the end of the summer, complete strangers would come up to me during various meetings and ask if I was the woman who was at such-and-such a museum just last week. Usually, my answer was yes, and the very kind stranger would say, "You really get around in that chair of yours!" But I digress.

Every Saturday morning, I would head out the front door of the dorm, decide the direction I wanted to go, and drive my chair in that direction until my battery was half full. Then I'd turn around and drive straight back to my dorm (usually with just enough juice in my battery to make it back to my dorm room). Along my way, I would stop at any museums, stores, parks, or statues that caught my attention. After taking the time to learn about the landmark or shop in the store, I'd continue on my journey.

Once I was in front of my dorm on my second Saturday in DC, I decided to turn right and drive in a straight line. I passed by a cute mall with one of my favorite restaurants in the world, Bertucci's, and many houses, stores, and various buildings. About 30 minutes into my jaunt, I approached a huge building with windows along the entire front, as high as I could see. I stopped in front of the building and looked through the middle pane of glass.

There was a photo exhibition in the lobby of this humongous building. I looked closer and realized that the subjects of the photos were blind children in Africa going about their day-to-day lives. It's pretty rare to simply see a photo exhibition featuring disabled people. Rarer still to see a photo exhibition of people with disabilities engaged in everyday activities—not tragic or "inspirational." Now you may be wondering, "Allison, when was the last time you saw a photo exhibition of Black people with disabilities simply living their lives?" Let me help you: never.

I was intrigued by the exhibition and the company that would feature these photos and had a sudden, strong desire to get inside of this mystery building to learn more. I looked up and read the name on the front: "World Bank." Looking into the window one last time, I thought, "I don't know how I'll do it, but I want to see that photo exhibit up close."

Since I majored in mathematical economics in college, I had studied the history and the policies of the World Bank. While my professors never overtly discussed the visitation policies of the World Bank, I knew that it wasn't a place that you just waltz into because you want to peruse a photo exhibition. You have to know someone who works there or have official business to be allowed inside. Since I had neither, I continued on my excursion.

While I spent my Saturdays exploring the city, I reserved Sundays for resting. My internship was fun, but physically tiring, and spending all day Saturday driving my wheelchair throughout the city was also a blast but depleted my body of energy the same way it depleted my chair's battery. So, at the beginning of the summer in DC, I committed myself to spending Sundays relaxing my muscles. However, by the second week of my internship,

I began to realize that I didn't need to rest all day on Sundays and I was longing to go to church. I had friends in my dorm who used public transportation to visit a new church in and around DC every week. They often invited me to go with them. While visiting a new church each week and spending time with my friends sounded great, I just didn't feel like that was the church experience I was looking for. I wanted to find a church that I could get to without public transportation.

Even in a city as accessible as DC, taking the public bus as a wheelchair user could be quite an adventure, because getting on and off buses required using a wheelchair lift—a process that can be tedious. However, not every bus had a working wheelchair lift and not every bus driver knew how to work it. So, when I took the bus, sometimes I had to wait for a wheelchair-accessible bus to be sent to the bus stop I was at. But it wasn't just the public transportation issue—on a deeper level I felt I wanted to go to the *same* church every week, to be a part of a community. Even though I was only going to be in DC for the summer, I still wanted to have a church home.

During my first Saturday jaunt in DC, I discovered Western Presbyterian Church—Western for short—which was located two blocks from my dorm. A week after realizing that I was craving a church home, I attended Western for the first time. The minister's sermon of embodying love and engaging in spiritually driven social service so resonated with me that I decided to attend Western every Sunday for the rest of the summer.

After a busy Saturday of sightseeing the day before and waking up earlier than normal to arrive at Western on time, I was ready to head to the dorm for a lovely nap after the service ended on my first Sunday. However, midway through getting my left arm into my jacket's sleeve, a woman approached me and asked, "Would you like to come to Fellowship Hall for some refreshments?"

I looked at her, so surprised and touched by the invitation that I put my plans for napping on hold and said, "Yes, I'd love to." She offered to help me finish putting my jacket on, and soon we were chatting as she walked with me to Fellowship Hall.

Once inside, I ended up having a wonderful time! As I sipped my water, various church members introduced themselves to me and asked questions about my studies and summer internship. Then one woman asked, "So tell me. What has been your favorite part of DC so far?"

Since I had just driven past the World Bank the previous week, this was an easy question to answer. I told her that I love being in a city that is the Mecca of policymaking. Just last week, I drove past the World Bank on my afternoon roll! I studied the policies of the World Bank for years as an economics major, and now to be living just blocks away from such an influential organization is, well, just awesome!

I continued on about how dedicated I was to using public policy to improve the lives of the disabled and how impressed I was by the World Bank's commitment to improving the lives of those living in extreme poverty and by the inclusive photo exhibition in the lobby of its building.

Once I finished talking, she smiled and said, "Allison, can you stay right here? I'll be right back."

I said okay, sipped my drink, and relaxed for a few moments.

The woman returned with a man and said, "Honey, I'd like you to meet Allison. She's getting ready to start her doctoral program in economics this fall and wants to use economic policy to help the disabled."

I smiled at the man who said hello and shook my hand.

"Allison, this is my husband, Jeff. He's worked at the World Bank for over 10 years and really enjoys his work."

Have you ever had the experience of seeing someone's lips moving and hearing words that are music to your ears, but you are certain there is absolutely no way that the person in front of you can be saying those words? That was me in that moment. It was about this time that I started hearing the theme music to *The Twilight Zone* in my head.

While I tried nonchalantly to compose myself, the woman was busy telling her husband how enamored I was with the World Bank.

Jeff turned to me and said, "I'd love to give you a tour of the bank and tell you about what we do."

By this time, I was certain that I was hallucinating this entire scenario! There was no way on God's green Earth that I drove by the World Bank one day and attended church eight days later, where I met someone who works at the bank, and they offered to give me a tour!

Once again, I had to nonchalantly compose myself. I excitedly agreed, and we exchanged e-mail addresses.

On my way back to my dorm, I was so excited by the possibility of touring the bank that I danced in my chair all the way. Although I had my chair on top speed, I felt like I was barely moving! I couldn't wait to get to my dorm room. As soon as I got home, I drove straight to my phone, called my mom, and told her the news, trying not to shout into her ear.

"That's wonderful! When do you go for the tour?" my mom asked with excitement filling her voice.

"I don't know yet. We have to work out the details. But, mom, this is *totally God*! There's no other explanation for this!"

"You're absolutely right, sweetie!"

Jeff and I sent e-mails to each other over the next few weeks, and we settled on a date and time for my tour. However, the day before the tour, I returned home from my internship to see that I had a message from Jeff. I did my best to stay calm as I opened the message. I was a bit nervous about its contents. What if he had to cancel?

I took a deep breath, opened the e-mail, and after reading the third sentence, I let out a loud scream for joy! Jeff e-mailed to see if I'd be able to extend my visit an extra hour. Knowing my dedication to disability policy, he had been able to secure a meeting for us with the World Bank's advisor on disability and development, Judy Heumann, the widely hailed mother of the disability rights movement! I couldn't speak, I was so excited! I wrote back as coherently as possible to say that I could stay as late as necessary. It's not every day that you receive the opportunity to have a one-on-one meeting with an absolute icon.

In case you are not familiar with her story: Judith "Judy" Heumann was born in 1947. She contracted polio at two years old and became a lifelong wheelchair user. Judy began her advocacy work in the 1970s when she sued the New York Board of Education for refusing to give her a teaching license due to her disability. She won the case and became the first wheelchair-using teacher in the state. Following this, she co-led a protest that shut down traffic in Manhattan to protest President Nixon's veto of the Rehabilitation Act and co-led a successful 26-day sit-in to push for the enforcement of Section 504, which prohibited discrimination by federally funded institutions against disabled people. Judy was also a key player in developing, implementing, and enforcing legislation such as the Americans with Disabilities Act, the Individuals with Disabilities Education Act, and the UN Convention on the Rights of Persons with Disabilities. She co-founded the Independent Living Movement, the Berkeley Center for Independent Living, and the World Institute on Disability. Later in her career, Judy served in the Clinton and Obama Administrations in addition to working at the World Bank. Her life is recounted in the critically acclaimed film *Crip Camp* (2020). Sadly, she passed away as this book was being written in 2023, but it will always mean so much that, amid all of her world-changing and paradigm-shifting work, Ms. Heumann agreed to take time out of her busy schedule to meet with me!

The next day came, and I, dressed in my sharpest suit, drove myself to the World Bank, went in the front door, and told the receptionist that I had official business there. As I waited for Jeff to come down from his office, the receptionist took my picture and issued me a World Bank day pass that she clipped onto my blazer. It was official: I was a guest of the World Bank.

A steady stream of people dressed in business suits was entering and leaving the building, and although people partially filled the lobby and the space echoed quite a bit, there was only a soft murmur of sound. The floor-to-ceiling windows that lined the front of the building let the sun's rays pour into the building, completely illuminating the entire space with natural light and a feeling of possibility.

"Hello, Allison! Are you ready for your day at the bank?" said Jeff as he walked toward me.

"Absolutely!" I said, trying to stay as calm as possible. After a magical day of touring the many departments and learning about this incredible place, Jeff and I arrived at Ms. Heumann's office. I was so excited to meet with her that I was actually calm! After our introductions, she invited us to take a seat near her desk. From this position, I had a front-row seat at the University of Judy Heumann, and Professor Heumann had a lot to teach. She gave us an overview of the World Bank's various projects to help the disabled in developing countries, then shared her vision how the bank should incorporate disability into its purview. She laid out the bank's past and current approach and how she was helping them evolve to reflect the diversity of the world's population.

I was inspired by her ability to be in full command of the details of day-to-day tasks of her current projects all over the world while also holding an overarching vision of the future of disability inclusion in development and a plan to help move the bank in the direction that would most benefit disabled people around the world. I saw firsthand just why Ms. Heumann was regarded as the mother of the disability rights movement in the United States.

While learning about her work at the bank was more than enough to satiate and inspire me, after teaching Jeff and me about disability and development, Ms. Heumann turned her attention to mentoring me. "So, Allison," she said. "Tell me about yourself and what you plan to do."

Excited and a bit shocked, that someone in Ms. Heumann's position wanted to hear about me, it took me a few seconds to switch from eager listener to a full participant in a discussion about my career. But after the surprise abated, I told her about how I'd been a disability rights advocate for as long as I could remember. I'd written letters to senators, met with congressmen, published articles, and written research papers to advocate for people with disabilities throughout my life. In high school, I discovered economics and chose to major in it in college. During college, I realized that I could use economics to help craft economically viable policies that would improve the employment rates of the disabled. So I decided to pursue a Ph.D. in economics and was admitted to MIT, where I was headed that coming September in just a few short weeks.

Ms. Heumann nodded her head in approval and asked, "Where do you see yourself working after grad school?"

"I'm not completely sure yet. I'd love to work on Capitol Hill here in DC or with a firm that advises congresspeople. I'm still figuring that out."

"That's okay. You have time. But if you want to work in DC on policy, you will need a much better wheelchair. We work very long hours, and you need to have a chair that will provide you with the proper support."

Once again, I was completely surprised by Ms. Heumann. I did not expect to receive career advice, let alone career advice that dealt with the practicalities of working as a disabled person. I assured Ms. Heumann that I did have a highly customized power wheelchair at home that provided me with the support that I needed.

She then asked, "Why don't you have it with you this summer?"

I explained that I'd seen a few of my friends' power wheelchairs broken during flights. So I only travel with my manual wheelchair when I fly. Thankfully, flying with my manual chair has always led to me landing in my destination with my wheelchair in working condition. However, I'm unable to push myself in my manual chair, so if I need a power wheelchair at my destination, I rent one for the duration of my trip. Since I needed independent mobility from the first minute I landed in DC, I just couldn't risk having a broken chair, even if that meant spending the summer in a chair that wasn't quite right for my body.

Most wheelchair users in the U.S. who have a disability as significant as mine, or Ms. Heumann's, have a wheelchair that is custom-b made for their bodies. Everything from the height and shape of the backrest to the material used for the seatbelt, to the density of the foam used in the seat cushion are determined by each person's individual needs. This level of specification ensures that each wheelchair user stays as healthy as possible, as independent as possible, and as active as possible. A poorly fitting wheelchair can lead to unnecessary health complications and hospitalizations.

After my explanation, Ms. Heumann nodded knowingly and went on to provide a myriad of suggestions regarding working in public policy with a disability. We discussed everything from securing punctual transportation to and from work to receiving personal assistance services during the workday. The conversation was illuminating and amazing! It was the first time that I received so much job advice that was tailored to both my career aspirations and my physical abilities.

After saying a grateful good-bye to Ms. Heumann, I gathered my belongings from Jeff's office and he escorted me to the lobby, where we began talking about the spark that initially lit my desire to come inside the bank: the photo exhibition. We went over to the photos, and he told me the story behind each photo. On my drive home, I thanked God for showering me with amazing blessings! As excited as I was to spend the day at the bank, I could have never, ever imagined having a day that was as awe-inspiring as that or the sequence of events that made it all happen.

Now, you may think that the story ends there. Oh no, there's more. Three years after that visit, I was in the thick of my doctoral studies at MIT. I was choosing classes for the fall semester of 2007, and there was only one class that would fit well in my schedule: development economics. But I wasn't so keen on taking it because, as far as I could tell, development economics had very little to do with my focus: labor economics and improving the employment rate of the disabled.

Why was this potentially a dealbreaker for me? you ask. Because I fancied myself a labor economist through and through. I have known since high school that one of the ways to ensure inclusion of people with disabilities in society is to shore up our economic situation, chiefly by improving our employment rate. Since labor economics is the study of everyone involved in the labor market—employers, employees, the self-employed, and the unemployed—and the factors (such as educational opportunities and on-the-job incentives) that impact employment outcomes, labor economics theories can be used to increase the percentage of disabled people who are employed. Combining labor economics theories with data analysis to understand the relationships between various inputs, such as new employment laws—and various outcomes, such as the average income of workers in a certain country—and seeing how those relationships change over time is unendingly fascinating to me. Thus, no other field of economics could capture my heart like labor . . . or so I thought.

However, I figured that I was in graduate school to expand my economics knowledge, and this was the only class that worked for my schedule, so I expanded out of my labor economics comfort zone and enrolled in development economics.

After the first week of class, I realized how wrong I was—I absolutely *loved* development economics! I enjoyed learning the theories, reading about pilot programs implemented throughout developing countries to improve the economic outcomes of the world's poorest poor, and learning new ways to use data analysis techniques. Simply put, I was hooked on the field. It also helped that two of the economics professors at MIT, Esther Duflo and Abhijit Banerjee, are leaders in the field and are enthusiastic about teaching the subject. Their enthusiasm and expert knowledge helped me to love the field.

Approximately halfway through the semester, I noticed that none of the academic papers we read for class discussed people with disabilities. I knew from previous research that disability is far more prevalent in developing countries than in developed countries and that disabled people are more likely to experience poverty than the nondisabled. These two facts suggested to me that development economics should be the mother ship of research on improving the economic outcomes of disabled people. Throughout the semester, I looked everywhere for academic papers in development economics that included disabled people and came up empty handed. So, once the fall semester ended, I met with Professor Duflo to ask her about the research on disability and development. She shook her head and said there was very little scholarship on the topic, and the research that had been done was quite cursory. She then hinted that I may think about adding my voice.

Before I left her office, the wheels in my head were already turning. I just had to figure out what data existed and how I could use the data to propel the field forward.

Instantly, it came to me: the World Bank had an entire division dedicated to disability and development!

The moment I returned to my dorm room, I got on my computer and looked up Ms. Heumann's contact information. After a few minutes of searching, it became clear that she was no longer at the World Bank. My heart sunk a bit, but then I remembered my other contact at the World Bank, Jeff. I looked for his business card in my book of business cards, but I couldn't find it. I sat for a moment and pondered my next move. I just knew that contacting the World Bank was the right step to take, but I wasn't sure of how to proceed. I sat quietly for a moment, and then it came to me. I decided to throw my version of a Hail Mary pass and simply sent an e-mail to the Disability and Development Team at the World Bank. I told them about my research interests and my academic background. Within hours, the coordinator of the team had responded to my e-mail and connected me to the senior economist on the Disability and Development Team.

Less than a month later, after speaking with the senior economist, I was asked to join a data-analysis team that was just beginning to analyze the results of a first-of-its-kind lending program to disabled people in India. I excitedly accepted the offer and worked on this project for the next 11 months. Upon completing my work for the World Bank, I was permitted to use the data to write a chapter of my dissertation. The chapter I wrote was so cutting-edge for the field that I was able to use it to get hired for my dream job a few months before completing my Ph.D.

Whenever I recount this story, I'm reminded of the importance of maintaining a spiritual practice "over the long haul," because you never know how God will arrange the synchronicities It has in store for you. Since the ultimate goal of the synchronicity often happens via a series of events, maintaining a spiritual practice long term is crucial to experience the fulfillment of the synchronicity. When I spent the summer in DC, I had zero interest in development economics. When Jeff gave me a tour of the World Bank, I simply thought that I was seeing a cool place and receiving phenomenal career advice that was tailored to me as a female wheelchair user who wanted to improve society for folks with disabilities. I had no idea that three years later, development economics would become one of my passions, and as a result, I would work for the World Bank, who would give me data for my dissertation and open up doors I didn't even realize I should be knocking on.

But what I did know was the importance of meditation and saying my morning and evening prayers. By meditating and praying every day, I regularly focused on my connection to God, tending that important relationship. Since God is all-knowing, by consistently tapping into my connection with It, I consistently tap into the all-knowing power of the Universe. When you tap into the all-knowing power again and again, you give it the opportunity to take a seed of a happy coincidence—i.e., coming across the World Bank—and grow it into a full-grown orchard of a synchronicity—i.e., receiving data from the bank that enables me to write a first-of-its-kind dissertation chapter and gain career experience doing uniquely rewarding work I wouldn't have pursued otherwise. As Rev. Michael Bernard Beckwith says, "Synchronicities give you an indication that there is a fundamental order in back of everything."[5] And as you spend more time in spiritual practice, you spend more time in the flow of this fundamental order, also known as Divine right order, which causes you to meet who you are supposed to meet, say what you are supposed to say, and think what you are supposed to think without any stress or strain on your part. All simply flows because you are in the ultimate flow: the flow of God.

Additionally, engaging in spiritual practices is crucial not only for recognizing and embracing synchronicity, but also for fully benefiting from synchronicity. We are able to take full advantage of synchronicities the more we take part in spiritual practices for a few reasons. Synchronicities are available to us all of the time, because God is active all the time, God is everywhere, and God loves us always—not just for one hour each Sunday. Synchronicities are just one of the many ways that God demonstrates Its love for us. Because God always loves us, It is always sending signals to tell us the best decision to make. However, we have to be aware, tuned in, and trust our intuition enough to guide us so we can fully benefit from the synchronicity.

Making the most of a synchronicity first requires us to recognize opportunities when they are presented to us. The more we engage in spiritual practices, the more present we become to each moment we are currently experiencing. Recognizing a synchronistic opportunity right in front of you is a challenge when your mind is preoccupied with thoughts about what you did last week, or who you have to text tomorrow, etc. However, when your mind is fully focused on the present moment, you can recognize opportunities that are yours to seize. The more you engage in spiritual practices, the more present you become to the current moment. When I visited Western Presbyterian Church for the first time, my plan was to go home immediately after the service and rest. However, when I was invited to Fellowship Hour by one of the parishioners,

I recognized that this was an opportunity to meet people and develop a church community. Now, I didn't know that going to Fellowship Hour would result in a life-changing experience. I simply seized the opportunity to meet people and allowed synchronicity to flow.

Additionally, engaging in spiritual practice makes you more receptive to your intuition. Fully benefiting from synchronicities usually requires taking action that may not make sense to the logical mind, that has no evidence of validity, and requires listening to a voice inside of you or a subtle feeling that tells you to take a certain action. This small voice or subtle feeling is your intuition speaking to you. When my development economics professor suggested that I conduct research that addressed the economic situation of disabled people in the developing world, I instantly knew deep down that, even though I did not have a current contact at the World Bank, I needed to reach out. So I followed that knowing, my intuition, and everything unfolded as it was supposed to. Since benefiting from synchronicities relies on us listening to our intuition, and our intuition is the voice of the Divine speaking to us, the more often we engage in spiritual practice, the more we benefit from synchronicity because we become more adept at hearing, understanding, and following our intuition.

Some may wonder if they have to know exactly what "the Divine plan" is for their lives in order to experience synchronicities. The answer to that is an emphatic no! In fact, even as we experience one synchronicity after another, we often have absolutely no idea of God's ultimate plan. We just know that we are presently experiencing synchronicities and living a life that is in sync with our greatest good. After all, as a new college graduate, I had absolutely no idea that I would write my doctoral dissertation on disabled people in India; I simply knew that I wanted to use economics to improve the lives of people living with disabilities, because ensuring the equal opportunities of disabled people brings me joy. Synchronicities occur when we have the desire to live according to the Divine plan for our lives, which is living a life that brings us authentic joy. We don't need to know everything. Indeed, God knows that our human minds cannot know everything. Some of us have difficulty determining what will bring us authentic joy, while others know what will bring them joy, but they don't know how to create opportunities for that joy to occur. This is where synchronicities can, and do, aid us in living the lives of our dreams. However, we must engage in spiritual practices to align ourselves with the Divine, because the more aligned we are with the Divine, the more in sync we are with the Divine plan. As you become more in sync with the Divine plan, synchronicities occur naturally to show you the best path for yourself.

Please bear in mind that not all synchronicities look like synchronicities. I've found that sometimes, synchronicities look like complete and utterly intractable roadblocks. These "incognito synchronicities" are actually guiding you to the path that will bring you the most joy, even when you think that a different path is the one you are meant to take. Hence, these synchronicities seem like they are preventing your happiness when, in reality, they are leading you to a happiness you never knew was yours. Such is the way I got my first big break in the acting industry.

I absolutely loved acting when I was little. I first discovered acting in kindergarten when I played a reindeer in my class's Christmas performance for our entire school. I just loved being onstage, delivering lines, and transporting myself, and the audience, to a made-up land for the duration of the show. It was magical . . . and fun.

From nursery school through second grade, I attended schools for kids with disabilities, so the fact that walking up and down the steps to the stage was not in my repertoire of skills and I spoke unclearly had no bearing on whether or not I could participate in school plays. The assumption was that there was a place onstage for every single student, regardless of disability. The teachers and school staff simply made changes to make sure that I, and every student in school, participated fully in every school production. Even when I enrolled in public school in third grade, I was always included in my class's school plays.

Since I only experienced inclusive theatrical school productions during my early childhood years, I grew up assuming that I would always be included in my schools' performances. Thus, on one January day, when my sixth-grade music teacher announced that the fifth and sixth graders would be performing selected scenes from *The Phantom of the Opera* for the school community, I was over the moon with excitement.

In addition to loving to act, I absolutely, positutely love musicals! *The Phantom of the Opera* was in the midst of a revival that year, which meant that almost every time I turned on the television, I saw the same commercial advertising tickets for the show. The commercial included a short snippet of the show's best-known song and ended with the iconic image of a half mask and a red rose. The ever-present ad heightened my interest in the show so much that I taught myself a few of the songs from the musical.

Hence the prospect of not only acting, but acting in *The Phantom of the Opera*, was almost too much for my 11-year-old self to handle. After announcing that the fifth and sixth graders would be performing the musical, my music teacher told us to see a specific staff member to sign up for auditions for the play.

Once class ended, I walked straight over to the staff member to sign up for auditions. He got out his clipboard, wrote down my name and contact information, and said he would be in touch to set up my audition. I knew I was on my way now! When I got home from school that day, I told my mom that I was going to audition for a musical and not just any musical: *The Phantom of the Opera.*

Now, I was your typical sixth grader. After signing up for my audition, my life got busy with science projects, memorizing dates for history class, learning theorems for math class, going to concerts with my youth group, and the biggest task of all . . . preparing for junior high school. I was one preteen with a full schedule, so the fact that the entire spring semester had come and gone and I had yet to audition for the musical completely escaped my attention. One day in May, I suddenly realized that I still had not auditioned. Since there were only a few weeks left of the school year, I figured that we were no longer doing the musical.

Just weeks after that realization, the day of my sixth-grade graduation came. I was all dressed up in a pretty white lace dress that my mother had picked out for me. I had been chosen to be a student speaker during the ceremony, so I was both excited and nervous to read my speech in front of the audience, which included the entire school community and the family of each graduating sixth grader.

The graduation ceremony was your typical sixth-grade graduation. The graduating students processed into the auditorium, onto the stage, and took our seats. School staff, teachers, and a few students gave speeches. The ceremony ended with each student receiving her or his diploma. Everything went like clockwork.

After we all received our diplomas, some of the sixth graders, including myself, left the stage to sit in the audience. I was so excited about graduating and receiving such a loud round of applause for my speech that I didn't notice over half of the graduating class was still seated onstage and most of the fifth graders were going up onstage.

"This is a curious turn of events," I thought to myself. "The stars of the show, us sixth graders, had already put on a spectacular graduation. What could possibly be happening now?"

A school staff member took a seat at the piano located next to the stage. As the lights in the auditorium went down, the teacher began to play the piano. By the third note, I knew what was happening. The musical that I wanted to participate in, that the teachers told us was open to all students, that I signed up to audition for, was about to take place with me sitting in the audience. I was absolutely crestfallen and had to use every bit of self-control not to cry.

At the end of the show, the teacher who promised to contact me to schedule my audition walked right past me. I stopped him and asked why he didn't include me in the audition for the show.

He said, "Oh yeah. I know you wanted to be in the show, but it would have been too hard to figure out how to get you onstage since we don't have a ramp. And your speech is so hard to understand that the audience wouldn't know what you were saying. Plus, you have to take a special bus to and from school, so I didn't think you would even be able to stay after school for rehearsals."

I was in complete disbelief at what he was saying and how nonchalantly he said it. My sadness began to turn into anger.

I replied, "But they figured out how to get me onstage for graduation, and you just have to call the bus company to tell them what time to pick me up. And you understand my speech."

He simply said, "It was just better this way. Being in the show probably would have been too much for you anyway. Congratulations on graduating and good luck in junior high." With that, he walked away.

And I was one livid 12-year-old! How dare he tell me what was for the best? And what right did he have to limit my opportunities to participate in extracurricular activities? I was a part of the student body and had just as much right to audition for a musical as every other student. By the time my mother found me to help me change out of my graduation attire into my school clothes, I'm fairly certain steam was shooting out of my ears and my face was a lovely shade of bright red.

My mom and I went to the girls' bathroom, and as soon as she had locked the door, I released a torrent of emotion.

"Mom, you know the play they did after the graduation ceremony?" I asked as my pretty white lace dress came off and my cute blue-and-pink jumper went on.

"Yes," said my mom.

"That's the play I wanted to try out for. But the teacher never told me when the auditions were so I never got to try out. I saw him today after graduation and I asked him why he didn't let me try out."

"What did he say?"

"He said it would have been too hard to have me in the play because my speech is too hard to understand and he didn't know how they'd get me onstage. But that stuff should not matter, Mom! There's always a way, but he just wouldn't try," I said in my preteen activist tone. "It just hurts that I didn't get a chance."

"I know it does. And you're absolutely right, sweetie. You should have been given the chance. But to the best of your ability, just let it go. There will be other opportunities for you to act onstage."

I knew my mother was right about the first part. I should have had the same chance as everyone else, but I was a bit dubious about her belief that there'd be other opportunities. This was the sixth-grade play, after all. Since I had just graduated from the sixth grade, what other opportunity could there be to be in the sixth-grade play? I wasn't quite sure that my mom fully understood the gravity of the situation. However, the play was over, and short of using the flying DeLorean from the movie *Back to the Future*, I didn't know of a way to change the past. So, once I finished changing clothes, I took a *very* deep breath and made the conscious decision to put the play behind me and enjoy my last day of elementary school.

A few weeks after the last day of sixth grade, I still felt a sting when I thought about the musical, but summer vacation was in full swing, which meant one thing for little Allison: summer camp was about to fill my days! I was beyond ecstatic! That summer, I attended Camp Echo Bridge for the first time.

Camp Echo Bridge was located in my town and was for kids with disabilities. The campers had everything from intellectual disabilities, to physical disabilities, epilepsy, albinism, and other conditions that I never learned. As you can imagine, having a camp filled with kids with such a wide range of gifts and abilities necessitated having counselors who were quite nimble in their approach to including everyone in every camp activity. One afternoon during the first week of camp, I was amazed when my counselors figured out how to fully include everyone on my team, which included me—one of two wheelchair-using campers—a camper who was legally blind, a camper who had a severe intellectual disability, and another camper with a phobia of balls in a fairly competitive game of kickball. The team we played against was composed of campers with equally diverse abilities, and yet every single camper participated, and we all had a blast.

So, when the counselors announced that we'd be performing *Cinderella* on the last day of camp, I was beyond excited because I knew that I'd be included in the play. My disability wouldn't be seen as a reason to exclude me; it would just be a part of the show, something to work with. I was assigned the role of the wicked stepmother. At first, I felt a little funny playing the wicked stepmother. But once we started rehearsals, I got into the role and found it was actually fun to play. The counselors gave me all sorts of ideas about how to move around the stage in my chair and continually reminded me to say my lines slower so the audience could understand me better.

In this case, my disability was not a hindrance to my performance—it became a part of my performance. Whenever I was conceiving something diabolical onstage, my counselors and I came up with a trademark spin that I would do in my chair. Since some of my lines included words that were especially challenging to understand, the counselors rewrote the script so that I'd be able to say these lines twice to give the audience extra time to understand my speech. The counselors wrote the lines to seem as though I was saying the same line twice for dramatic effect, but in reality, it was an accommodation.

My experience with the sixth-grade play became a distant memory as I fully immersed myself in this experience, into the feeling of being wanted onstage and praised for my acting abilities. I was fully present to the moment and felt immense gratitude for being fully included.

After weeks of rehearsal, the day had come for the curtain to rise for Camp Echo Bridge's debut performance of *Cinderella*. As community members and families and friends of the campers filled the seats of the auditorium, campers were backstage excitedly waiting as our stage manager began the countdown. Adrenaline was pumping through my 12-year-old body as I waited to roll out on the stage.

After what seemed like an eternity, our stage manager gave the cue, and our camp director went onstage to welcome the audience members. Then, a counselor raised the curtain, and it was time to show our families, friends, and community members just what a group of disabled kids can do when given the chance to grace the stage.

In the interest of complete transparency, some of the details of the show escape my memory; however, I do remember the first time I did my trademark spin to show that I was hatching a diabolical plan. The crowd went wild! They laughed so loudly that I had to wait for them to quiet down to deliver my next line. I felt so alive and electric on that stage. I absolutely loved the feeling of holding the audience in the palm of my hand and feeling the audience's energy. The audience laughed at all of my one-liners, so I was pretty sure that they could understand my speech. I was in joyful rapture on that stage.

Before I knew it, we reached the end of the play, and the cast was taking its bow. After the curtain went down, all of the counselors came onstage to tell the campers what a great job we did. Although my body was pulsating with energy from the joy of being onstage, I still managed to ask a counselor if she thought people could understand me.

"Allison, are you kidding? You stole the show! Everyone could understand you just fine!" was her response.

Once all of the campers were out of costume, we gathered on the side of the stage and went outside to meet our families on the camp's grassy field to have a picnic. My counselor helped me find my mom among the throngs of people. As my mom and I settled down on the field to eat lunch with all of the other campers and families, person after person came up to me to say how much they enjoyed my performance.

One person said that I had "a real knack for acting and should keep it up!"

Moments later, another person said, "I will never look at someone turning their wheelchair in the same way again" as they chuckled.

I was astonished by the positive reactions to my performance and asked my mom, "Was I really that good?"

"Oh, honey! You were great up there!" she said, giving me a big kiss.

"Mom, I want to act more. It's so much fun! Maybe I can try out for a play at my new school," I said.

Just five weeks later, I was officially a junior high student. About two months into my first year of junior high, I was doing homework in my living room when the phone rang. My mom answered and was engaged in a conversation that seemed to have nothing to do with me, so I kept doing my homework.

However, five minutes later my mom's head peeked out from the kitchen. She said, "Allison, would you like to audition to be in a children's movie?"

I stopped doing my homework, raised my head, and stared blankly at my mom for a second, not believing my ears, and then screamed, "YES! YES! When's the audition?"

My mom told the person on the phone that I was quite definitely interested. She wrote down all of the information and hung up the phone.

"Mom, who was that?" I asked, nearly bouncing off the walls with excitement.

Mom explained that she had just been speaking with the director of our city's department of parks and recreation, who had recently received a phone call from the casting director of Kidvidz, a company based in our town that made children's movies and distributed them nationwide. They were preparing to film their next movie and wanted to include child actors with disabilities, so they contacted her to see if she knew of any local disabled kids who would like to audition. Since she attended the play I did with Camp Echo Bridge, she instantly thought of me!

I was absolutely astonished! At the end of sixth grade, I was excluded from auditioning for a play because I had a disability. Now, in the seventh grade, I received an opportunity to audition for a movie, in part, because I had a disability!

A few weeks after that phone call, my mom took me to audition for *Paws, Claws, Feathers & Fins*—a movie about pet care. On a late autumn afternoon, we arrived at a large building that looked like a warehouse from outside. I was a tad nervous, until my mom pushed me in my pink-and-black wheelchair through the front door and we immediately entered a huge room. My nervousness momentarily transformed into disbelief about the scene unfolding there.

The room was teeming with parents and kids. Parents were quietly sitting in wooden folding chairs along the walls of the room, waiting for their child's name to be called. The kids were running around, playing games with each other, throwing balls across the room, and talking as loudly as humanly possible, or so it seemed. I just sat in the doorway for a moment, taking in the general chaos that was the audition waiting room.

After signing in, we found a spot to sit and, well, sat until someone called my name. While we waited, my mom put on her headphones and began meditating.

I was so focused on figuring out how my mom could meditate in this noisy, crowded room that my nervousness about the audition dissipated until I heard, "Allison Thompkins. Where's Allison Thompkins?" I waved my hand at the clipboard-holding woman calling my name.

Once she saw me, she came over to me and asked if I'd like some help getting to the audition room. I said yes.

As she pushed me into the back room, we chatted. I kept thinking, "Oh boy! Here we go. Just stay cool, Allison. You've got this!"

Before I knew it, I was parked right in front of a fairly large camera, and the director of the movie was telling me what to expect. "Okay, Allison. We're just going to ask you a few questions and then say a few lines that we'd like you to repeat back to us. Just say the lines like you would in the movie. Okay?"

After about 20 minutes of questions and interpreting lines and a roller coaster of nervousness and excitement, I finished my audition and was pushed back to my mom.

"How did it go?" asked my mom.

"It was so much fun! I was nervous at first; but then I just relaxed into it," I said, quite proud of myself for completing my first audition for a professional acting job.

I did my best to put the audition out of my preteen mind, but I met with varying levels of success as the waiting game began. Some days, I completely forgot that I had even auditioned. Other days, knowing that the casting director would call me to notify me of the casting decision, I kept picking up the phone all day long, just to make sure our phone had a dial tone . . . it always had one.

One day, I came home from school and was greeted by a message on our answering machine. This was one of the days when I had completely forgotten about the audition, so when I listened to the message saying I had gotten a part in the movie, I ran around our house screaming in sheer delight! I won't say how many times I almost fell during my very vociferous celebration, but suffice it to say that my mom, who was celebrating with me, strongly urged me to sit down while I screamed and squealed for joy.

A few months later, on a beautiful spring day during my April vacation, I arrived at the site of the filming of my scene of the movie. The scene was being filmed on a bike path next to a river in Boston. Since I was the first one to arrive at the site, I sat quietly and collected myself. I had such an interesting combination of sensations coursing through my body that I needed a moment to just be. On one hand, I was so excited to be moments away from acting in my first movie that I felt like I was floating above my body. On the other hand, I was keenly aware of the present moment and was determined to remain focused on the task at hand so that I did a wonderful job.

As I sorted through the range of emotions and sensations I was experiencing, the director, the videographer, and the woman who pushed me into the audition room all those months ago arrived at the bike path. When we saw each other, we greeted each other like long-lost friends. It was such a welcoming environment that I was even more excited to dive into the acting. While talking to the three adults, I noticed another member of our group: a teenage girl who was holding the leash of a full-grown golden retriever.

After being formally introduced to the girl, the director explained the scene to me, told me my lines, and showed me the general movements he wanted me to make. I was to appear in the movie with the golden retriever. On the surface, this seemed like a perfectly reasonable, even logical, request. After all, this was a movie about kids taking care of pets. However, while I loved most animals, I was deathly afraid of dogs at the time.

This fear began when my family and I arrived at my grandparents' house for our annual summer visit when I was five years old. My grandparents had a dog, a rather large dog as I remember it. Now I admit, as a five-year-old, any dog bigger than a toy poodle was huge to me. But I digress. My family and I had finally arrived after an eight-hour drive, and I had just gotten out of my parents' car. My sister was in the process of handing me my crutches when my grandparents' dog jumped up on me and knocked me over. My head struck the floor of my grandparents' carport hard, resulting in a sizable bump on my head and a massive headache. Prior to that incident, I was ambivalent about dogs. After that incident, I was absolutely terrified of them. I was certain they were all uncontrollable beasts that would hurt me, so I wanted nothing to do with them.

Of course, I told the director none of this. I knew that if I wanted to make my film debut, I was going to have to get over this fear . . . and fast. After all, the show—or children's movie as the case may be—must go on. Thankfully, before we started filming my scene, the director gave the dog and me a few minutes to get to know each other. I just petted the dog, and the more I stroked his fur, the closer he came to me. Eventually, the dog put his little face on my lap and seemed to be enjoying the contact as much as I was.

Since I didn't feel comfortable talking out loud to the dog, I started talking to the dog in my head by saying, "Okay, little dog. I'm kind of scared of you, but we have to be in this movie together. So please don't make any sudden moves, and I promise to keep petting you. We're in this together."

While I was mentally conversing with my co-star, the director and cinematographer were determining the best backdrop for my scene and asking bystanders to steer clear of the set.

Before I knew it, I heard, "Okay, Allison. Are you ready for the first take?"

I was so excited that I momentarily forgot about my fear of my co-star, let out one of my trademark Allison squeals, and said, "Oh yeah!"

After chuckling a bit, the director pushed me to the place he wanted me to be, sat the dog next to me, and checked the view from the video camera. Once he was pleased with the visual composition of the scene, he yelled, "Action!"

I was surprised that he actually said the word *action*. I had a brief out-of-body experience. Here I was—a 12-year-old with cerebral palsy (CP) who used a wheelchair part-time, drooled, had a speech disability who was less than a year removed from being excluded from a school play because of the CP and who was on the precipice of acting in a children's movie that would be distributed nationally! I took a moment just to acknowledge this internally.

However, knowing that I had a job to do, I returned to my body and delivered my lines with all of the gusto of about 1,000 preteens. I was having a blast!

We had done about three takes when the director said, "You're delivering the lines beautifully, Allison, but can you interact with the dog more? Maybe pet him before you start talking, or look at him and then look up at the camera?"

"Sure!" I replied.

As I said it, I was thinking, "If only this director knew just how much I've overcome to simply sit next to this dog without undoing the wheel locks on my chair and rolling away at top speed screaming 'get that dog away from me!'"

But of course, I was a professional. So, I took a deep breath, thought of how I could interact with the dog more, and gave the signal that I was ready for the next take. We did the scene a few more times. Each time, I thought of a different way to interact with my co-star as I said my lines, looking down at him as I stroked him and rested my arm on his back.

After about five more takes, I heard a very happy director say, "I think we've got it! Now, Allison, we want to get footage of you just petting and playing with the dog."

By this time, I was quite comfortable with my co-star, so I genuinely loved petting him. Petting his thick, soft fur was actually relaxing, and it felt really good to my usually tight, clenched hand, a symptom of CP. After a few minutes of playing with the dog on camera, I heard, "That's a wrap."

I couldn't believe it! I had just finished my very first acting job, and now I was less afraid of dogs. Who knew that by fulfilling one of my dreams, I would also release a fear and see the beauty of one of God's creations? I was by no means ready to own my own dog; however, from that day on I began pushing myself to interact with dogs more, especially golden retrievers, who still have a special place in my heart to this day.

Although I didn't know the word *synchronicity*, I knew that I had just finished my first acting gig because I had released the disappointment of being excluded from one opportunity, which enabled me to fully reveal my gifts while embracing the joy of being included in another opportunity. By engaging in meditation, revealing the fullness of my gifts, and choosing to be joyful, I remained in constant alignment with the Divine, which increased my receptivity to the flow of the synchronistic unfolding of events.

When I was excluded from the sixth-grade play, I could have quit my daily meditation practice. After all, what I thought I truly wanted was "withheld" from me, and if God is God, surely It could have orchestrated events so I could participate in the play. However, I wanted to be in the sixth-grade play because I never fathomed that I would have the opportunity to be in a children's movie. Although I loved acting and daydreamed about becoming a professional actor in front of the camera, appearing in a children's movie was not on my radar as being remotely possible. I didn't live in Hollywood. I didn't have an agent or headshots. So, at age 12, I thought the crème de la crème was being in my school play.

However, God is ever-expanding, ever-unfolding, and always seeking to give us our authentic desires and to propel us further along our journey of growth and evolution. By continuing to meditate regularly, I kept myself in alignment with this ever-expanding and ever-unfolding energy of generosity and love. Since I had been in school plays before, the time had come for me to expand my horizons by acting in a brand-new medium, a medium that I wanted to try but had zero idea of how to access.

And not only was it time for me to realize my dream of being in a movie, but it was also time for me to share my love of acting with more people than just my school community. I was to act in this movie not only for myself, but also for the kids around the country who would watch the movie. Who knows if another little one in a wheelchair or with a speech disability saw that movie and realized that they could be an actor too? We never know how the Divinely created opportunities that we seize will improve the world.

But, to experience the opportunity of being in a movie, I had to release the disappointment that stemmed from the sixth-grade play. Some might have understood if I had remained angry about being excluded and taken that anger with me to Camp Echo Bridge. Others might have agreed with me if I said that "this camp play is no big deal. I'm not going to give it my all because it's not important." However, either one of those mindsets would have blocked the synchronicity of the opportunity to act in a children's movie because I would have failed to live in the truth of my being, which is joy and sharing my gifts in their fullness. When things happen that anger or disappoint us, fully and healthfully feeling those emotions is critical so we can release them. When we perpetually feel angry or sad, we close ourselves off from God's natural proclivity to reveal the opportunities It has for us. Opportunities that can arise from the most unexpected places.

At the time I was invited to audition for the movie, I lived in a suburb of Boston known more for being an excellent school district than for being a hotbed of filmmaking. And yet I received the opportunity to act in a movie being filmed right in my neighborhood. This opportunity came because I seized the opportunity to act in my camp's play. By revealing the fullness of my gifts, I was living in the fullness of God because God gave me the gift to act. When you allow your gifts to shine through you, you allow God's very presence to reveal Itself through you and to be palpable right where you are, which creates the energy within and around you for synchronicities to occur.

HOW TO LIVE IN SYNCHRONICITY

Exercises and Prompts

Since synchronicity is one of the gifts of engaging in spiritual practice, we cannot engage in synchronicity like we engage in prayer or meditation, but we *can* engage with synchronicity and create an atmosphere around ourselves that ushers more synchronicity into our daily lives. As Deepak Chopra writes, "The power of intention is a critical factor in all areas of life. Simply by intending to create synchronicity in your life, you can nurture that result."[6]

Exercise 1: Recognizing a synchronicity when one occurs is one of the most potent ways to engage with synchronicities.

Sometimes when events happen that seem magical or highly unlikely, we call the occurrences a coincidence or uncanny. When we choose to see a synchronicity as mere happenstance rather than seeing it as the love of God orchestrating events for our ultimate happiness, we move ourselves out of alignment with God and we miss an opportunity to deepen our conscious connection with, and expand our awareness of, God. So labeling synchronicities as synchronicities is the first way to engage with them and to increase the number of synchronicities you experience.

Exercise 2: Express gratitude for the synchronicities you experience.

Create a synchronicity journal where you keep a record of all the synchronicities you experience. When you experience a synchronicity, make a note of it in your synchronicity journal. Later that day, or whenever you have time, set a timer for between two and five minutes and say aloud how grateful you are for the synchronicity that you experienced and why you are grateful until your timer goes off. When doing this exercise, feel grateful at the deepest level of your being. Expressing and feeling gratitude for something brings more experiences of that something into your life. See my Gratitude chapter for a discussion of this.

Exercise 3: Strengthen your intuitive muscles.

Following your intuition is a key part of experiencing synchronicities. Below are a few intuition sharpening exercises.

a. If you receive a text or phone call, before you look to see who is calling or texting you, intuit or guess who is contacting you.

b. If you are waiting for an elevator and there is more than one elevator, guess which elevator will be the one you will take.

c. Before opening your e-mail account, guess how many new e-mails you have.

d. Every time you guess correctly, celebrate! You can silently say, "Way to go, intuition! Awesome job!" Or something similar. Don't worry if you initially guess incorrectly. Your intuition is like a muscle. It will get stronger the more you use it.

Exercise 4: Meditate on the signs.

If you have been experiencing synchronicities, such as seeing the same color or the same sequence of numbers or hearing the same name repeatedly, but you don't know what it means or what action you should take, meditate. I recommend doing a Transcendental meditation session (see the Meditation chapter for details on this type of meditation). The steps for this follow.

a. Set a timer for anywhere from 10 to 30 minutes.

b. Sit quietly. Mentally ask God to reveal what you should do in relation to the synchronicity you are experiencing.

c. Choose your own mantra or use one of the following mantras: love, clarity, or understanding.

d. Close your eyes and say the mantra in your mind each time you inhale and each time you exhale for the duration of your meditation.

e. If your mind begins to wander as you meditate, that's okay. When you become aware that your mind is wandering, simply return your attention to your breath and your mantra.

f. Once you finish your meditation, sit quietly for between 10 and 60 seconds.

ACCESS NOTES

Exercise 2: Express gratitude for the synchronicities you experience.

1. *If you want to express gratitude for synchronicities that you experience, and you are unable to speak,* try the following.

   a. Make note of the synchronicities you noticed. Whenever you have time, set a timer for between two and five minutes and do one of the following:

      i. Think about how grateful you are for the synchronicity that you experienced.

      ii. Write down why you are so grateful for the synchronicity or type it into the software you use for writing.

   b. If typing and writing are challenging, instead of writing complete sentences, type or write one or two words that sum up each reason you are grateful (for example, instead of typing "I'm grateful for this synchronicity because it made me laugh," write or type "laughter." Instead of writing "This synchronicity makes me thankful because it made my life easier," write or type "ease"). When doing this exercise, feel grateful at the deepest level of your being.

Exercise 3: Strengthen your intuitive muscles.

2. *If you are blind or have low vision,* you can do the following intuition-strengthening exercises:

    a. Before opening your e-mail account, guess how many new e-mails you have.

    b. If you use paratransit, guess how many stops the vehicle will make before you arrive at your destination.

Exercise 4: Meditate on the signs.

3. *If you would like to meditate on the meaning of a synchronicity you are experiencing, but Transcendental meditation does not work for you,* try the following steps.

    a. Do your typical premeditation routine.

    b. Silently say the following statement: "Universe, please tell me the meaning of such-and-such synchronicity."

    c. Do your usual meditation.

CHAPTER FIVE

meditation

Meditation is a way for nourishing and blossoming the divinity within you.[1]

— AMIT RAY

Have you ever been in the presence of a friend or family member who promises that she is listening to you recount a story as she cleans her home, checks her social media, and prepares lunch for you two, and at the end of your story, when you ask her what she thinks you should do, she looks at you blankly and says, "About what?" Although you were speaking to the person directly and clearly, they were completely oblivious to absolutely everything you said.

Many times, God has a similar experience with us—we are the oblivious friend. God is everywhere and is always sending messages to us through our intuition, hunches, gentle nudges, inspired thoughts, and the like; but, to perceive and understand the messages that God is broadcasting, which is God's voice, we must spend focused, uninterrupted time with God. To understand this better, think of a radio station. A radio station is always broadcasting music or news or whatever is on the radio these days, but the only people who hear what the station is broadcasting are people who have their radio tuned to the correct number on the dial. If a station broadcasts at 108 FM, but your radio is tuned to 94 FM, you will miss everything that the station is broadcasting. The same is true with God. God is always broadcasting signals for us to pick up; however, we have to tune our radios—ourselves—to the correct station to receive and understand the messages God is sending.

Meditation is a way for us to tune in to God's radio station, or God's frequency, because meditation aligns us with God. As you increase your alignment with God, you become more in sync with God, which enables your spirit, mind, and body to tune in to God's frequency and "hear" the messages It is broadcasting.

When we meditate, we block out the stimulus of the world and focus within, which is the genesis and bedrock of our relationship with God. This focus causes the qualities of God—such as love, joy, abundance, intelligence, generosity—to become increasingly active in our thoughts, feelings, and behavior and in the external circumstances of our lives. Our thoughts, feelings, and actions become increasingly infused with the qualities of God. And as we meditate, we are not only focusing on God, but we are also communing with God. When we commune with God, we experience our oneness with God. As we spend more time feeling our unity with God, we increasingly behave from that unity in our daily lives, thereby becoming the qualities of God that we often seek.

Meditation entered my life the summer I was eight years old. That summer turned out to be pivotal for me, but I had no idea how important it was until years later. I was too busy riding my bike, playing with my sister and our friends, and trying to get my parents to give me as much ice cream and bubble gum as humanly possible. In the midst of all of this childhood fun, my mother began attending a new church, Plymouth Church of Shaker Heights, where the senior minister was Rev. Dr. William Holliday. Although his official name was Rev. Holliday, he went by the nickname Skip. I always got a kick out of being able to call an adult—especially a minister—Skip. One of the spiritual practices that Skip did himself, and taught his parishioners to do, was centering prayer. I learned in later years that centering prayer is another name for Transcendental meditation.

My mom was one of Skip's committed students, and the fact that she began doing centering prayer on a daily basis meant exactly one thing for eight-year-old me: *I* learned how to do centering prayer. Centering prayer, or Transcendental meditation, is a practice in which you choose a word or phrase, and you think this word or phrase, which is called a mantra, each time you inhale and each time you exhale. You keep your eyes closed and sit up as straight as you can while remaining comfortable and relaxed. Although my mom did centering prayer every day for at least 40 minutes, since I was only eight, she taught me to do it five days per week for as close to 15 minutes as I could handle.

I have to admit, initially I felt this whole centering prayer thing was a bit . . . okay, *very* boring. I mean, all you did was just sit there and think the same thing over and over and over again. Surely, there was something else I could do that would have the same desired effect but had a little more pizzazz to it. However, the more I meditated, the more I noticed that my life seemed to flow a little easier. Once I became adept at meditating for 15 minutes five days per week, my mom upped the ante and said that I needed to meditate seven days per week for 30 minutes each day. This felt a bit daunting at first, but over time I got used to it and eventually came to look forward to my meditation sessions.

Like any child would, I had periods when I engaged in centering prayer every day for 30 minutes each day, and then I would go through periods when I didn't meditate for weeks. However, I'd always eventually return to the practice because, even as a child, I found life would somehow just move more naturally and more miraculously when I was meditating daily. It wasn't until I was about 19 or 20 years old that I made the commitment to meditate every day. Sometimes this meant spending 10 minutes in meditation, and sometimes this meant spending over one hour in meditation, but I did it every day.

By my first day as a professional economist, I was a devoted Transcendental meditator. I meditated daily for at least 20 minutes, and I tried to meditate for 45 minutes as much as possible.

One September day in 2011, I dressed in my sharpest suit and arrived for my first day of work at Mathematica, a company dedicated to improving society through actions such as data collection and analysis, writing reports, overseeing and analyzing pilot programs that become government policy, and proposing public policies for clients such as the U.S. Department of Nutrition and USAID. I was incredibly excited, nervous and, most of all, eager to start my career as an economist.

As soon as I was settled into my office on the eighth floor, my new colleague, Josh, took me on a tour so I could learn the layout of the building and meet as many colleagues as possible. After trying to commit the 25th name to my memory in about 30 minutes, I realized that if I kept trying to do this, steam was going to start coming out of my ears from overloading my memory circuits. So, for the remainder of the tour, I just enjoyed meeting people and resolved to learn my colleagues' names over the course of a few weeks rather than a few seconds.

At 1:00 P.M. on that first day, Josh and I went to a huge conference room, where we joined staff members from our office as well as staff members from every Mathematica office around the country who held the same position I had or higher. This was my first meeting of this kind, and it felt a bit surreal.

I was prepared just to sit back and observe, but I was in for a surprise when, after a few minutes, my supervisor, Brian, leaned close to the phone and told the entire company that this was my first day at Mathematica and gave everyone a brief description of my background and research interests. I was a bit, okay *quite*, embarrassed and could feel blood rush to my cheeks. Fortunately, my colleagues in the room smiled at me during the introduction, which helped me relax . . . a little.

Mathematica fulfills its mission of mitigating social challenges from climate change to the underemployment of people with disabilities through a variety of data-driven activities for a wide range of clients. Each of Mathematica's clients proposes a project that Mathematica bids on. If Mathematica wins the bid, Mathematica employees who have the technical expertise and subject matter knowledge pertinent to the project are staffed on that particular project.

When you are a new employee, you are staffed on any project that needs additional support. In this way, new staff members learn about subjects outside of their field of expertise and get to know how various departments within the company function.

During my first few weeks, I was staffed on multiple projects, including two projects in the education field and one project pertaining to disability policy. Although I had only studied education as it applied to disabled young adults, I quickly learned a whole set of analytical skills and became quite knowledgeable about the issues within education policy that were pertinent to my projects.

One of the education projects that I was staffed on required creating a data-based system to analyze the effectiveness of teachers across a school system. Initially, my role on that project was to attend biweekly teleconferences where I would listen to the conversation, take notes, and follow up on the tasks that needed to be completed. After a few meetings and reading tons of articles on teacher evaluation, I asked the occasional question regarding the available data and validity of certain variables during meetings. After a month or so, the project leader and my supervisor, Brian, began asking me to take the lead on guiding the discussion and answering the client's questions during our teleconferences in addition to carrying out all the analysis activities outlined in our contract with the client.

After I led a few meetings independently, Brian asked me to speak with him on the telephone.

"Allison, I'd like you to become project leader of the teacher evaluation project. I'll take care of the budgeting and staffing, and you'll continue working with the client, delegating tasks to other Mathematica staff working on the project, and overseeing all of the deliverables. What do you think?" Brian asked.

He shared that he had talked to the client after each meeting I led, and they were pleased with how responsive

I was to their concerns and how adept I was with the analysis. They also told him what a pleasure I was to work with.

Thus, I became the project leader and became responsible for the day-to-day activities needed to fulfill our contract with the client. It was amazing to see my own professional growth on just one project.

This was the pattern I experienced on almost all of the projects that I was staffed on during my first year at Mathematica. I would join the project at the entry level for someone with a Ph.D., and over time the senior staff on the project would teach me new skills related to working with clients or writing for a public policy audience or any other skill necessary for professional success. As I learned each skill, I was given more responsibilities on the project.

In my second year, I was chosen to be one of the Principal Investigators on a brand-new project for the Social Security Administration. This meant that for the first time I would co-lead a project from its inception to its completion. This was incredibly exciting, and it reflected my growth and my colleagues' confidence in my work. In addition to this new role, I was publishing quite a few papers and being invited to speak at conferences and lead discussions regarding disability policy research. As I worked on more projects, my colleagues were requesting that I be staffed on their projects increasingly. So much so, that my supervisor occasionally had to take me off a few projects because I was staffed for more hours than I was available.

As much as I loved the work I was doing, the people I worked with also made my workday enjoyable. Often, a trip to the office supplies room would turn into a conversation about the local sports team, or watching a video of someone trying a new activity the previous weekend, or explaining just why purple is the best color in my book.

Going to the water cooler would inevitably turn into an opportunity to chat with someone about a new project they had just been staffed on. We had trick-or-treating on Halloween so staff members who wanted to have their children come to the office after school would be greeted by Mathematica employees who had candy at their desks. We held parties for Pi Day, celebrated staff members' Mathematica anniversaries, and genuinely cared for each other. If a colleague experienced a crisis, Mathematica staff would rally together to provide whatever support we could.

I had temperature and respiratory needs related to cerebral palsy (CP) that the entire eighth floor was not wired to meet. However, my office was modified to meet those needs, which meant spending time in areas outside of my office wasn't always healthy for me. So my colleagues would often come by my office just to say hi and chat for a bit.

While I absolutely reveled in the atmosphere and community of Mathematica's office and I was excelling professionally, the state of my health was a completely different story. When I was interviewing for the job, I discussed my ideal work schedule with Human Resources and negotiated working full-time and working from home two and a half days per week. I knew that working full-time would require quite a bit of energy but reasoned that working from home halftime would enable me to conserve a great deal of energy.

Well, by the end of my first month, I was beyond exhausted. On the days I went into the office, I was so tired by the time I got home at the end of the day, I couldn't speak and could barely hold my head up. Fortunately, I had phenomenal caregivers who learned alternative ways of communicating with me in the evenings, and

I had a headrest on my wheelchair that could hold up my head for me. However, I was not accustomed to being this exhausted every day, and it was disconcerting.

I spoke with a few mentors who assured me that feeling tired during your first few weeks of a new job was completely normal. They told me that my body has to adjust to the rhythm of my new job. And once I've acclimated to the job, the exhaustion that I was experiencing would recede and my muscle control would return to my normal.

This sounded wonderful to me. So I did the best I could to manage the extreme fatigue I felt on the days I went into the office by literally staying in bed all day on the weekends and whenever I had a day off from work. Although I was resting as much as I could while I waited for my body to adjust to my work schedule, the fatigue in my body became more and more intense. Instead of feeling better, I felt worse, and my health was beginning to decline. By my fourth month of working at Mathematica, I had developed a persistent cough and was having weekly asthma attacks and difficulty speaking throughout the day.

Since I enjoyed the work I was doing and was committed to figuring out how to continue working while maintaining my health, I sought help from my physician, who put me on a few medications. After a month on these new prescriptions, the weekly asthma attacks escalated into asthma attacks two or three times per week, and the cough worsened as the fatigue in my body continued to increase.

After months of trying to get my body to bend to the will of my mind and hearing my body repeatedly say, "Listen, woman, I done told you what I needed to be healthy and you keep ignoring me, so I'm going to throw more health complications your way until you get the message," I finally got the message.

I knew that the severe fatigue and ill health I was experiencing were due to putting my body under more stress than it could handle. By early 2013—around halfway through my second year at Mathematica—I realized that I had to decrease the load on my body. No dose of medication was going to heal the exhaustion that had become a near-permanent state. I needed to create a work schedule that honored my physical needs. I knew what I needed to do, but I was hesitant to actually do it. What if I lost the job I loved? What if I no longer got to enjoy the fun atmosphere of Mathematica's office? What if? What if? These "what if's" filled my mind until I forced my mind to cease thinking those thoughts. I took a deep breath and thought, "What if I do irreparable harm to my body by continuing to work like this?"

With the last "what if" at the forefront of my mind, I summoned the courage to schedule a meeting with Brian to discuss adjusting my work schedule. To my absolute delight and relief, Brian approved my request to work four days per week and to work from home exclusively. Brian also expressed concern about my health and offered to do anything he could to help. I was incredibly thankful to work at Mathematica but also sad that I would no longer be in the office.

Of course, I knew that I needed to take better care of my body, rest more, and remove the stress of commuting to and from the office. Working from home allowed me to do all of this and so much more. But working from home also meant I would no longer be able to joke with Josh as he walked by my office, or trade information about the newest disability service in the Boston area with one of my disabled colleagues as we waited for the elevator, or chat with my colleagues as we waited for the weekly company-wide meeting to begin. In short, while I'd continue to be able to do the work I loved, I'd miss the social interaction of the office.

After a few months of working from home exclusively, my health began to improve! The first week I went without an asthma attack, I celebrated by ordering my favorite meal from my favorite restaurant. It was a monumental week. Although I still had a persistent cough, it had lessened.

Throughout all the health complications I experienced, I continued doing Transcendental meditation every day. I knew that my meditation practice enabled me to produce the high quality of work that I did even though my health was not so great. However, during the summer of 2013—nearly two years after that first day in this high-intensity job—I began to research other ways to meditate.

Transcendental meditation was still my go-to practice, but doing this type of meditation was becoming harder due to changes in my ability to control my breathing, increased muscle spasms, and constant coughing. Since Transcendental meditation requires you to focus on thinking a word or phrase with every inhalation and exhalation, every time I coughed, I lost my focus. Since I didn't have smooth inhalations and exhalations, trying to time my mantra to my breath became a guessing game. I spent more time trying to figure out how to time my mantra with my variable breathing pattern than in meditation. When my timer signaled the end of my meditation session, I felt more frustrated and fatigued than relaxed. I felt like I had spent 30 minutes trying to tame my muscles rather than focusing on my oneness with the Divine. The meditation that had been so effective for me since my childhood felt like an impossible challenge now. Although

Transcendental meditation reminded me of the increased challenges I was facing with controlling my muscles, I knew that there had to be another way for me to meditate easily even with the changes in my body.

So I searched the Internet and enrolled in online meditation classes. In each class, I learned about different types of meditation. Most importantly, I tried forms of meditation that I never heard of and discovered two forms of meditation that worked brilliantly for me: Tapping meditation and guided meditation.

I had immediate success with Tapping meditation (or Tapping). Simply put, Tapping felt incredible. After my first time Tapping, I felt more relaxed and like I had released some of the tension that had built up in my body. Tapping is a meditation technique where you literally tap on different parts of your body associated with certain meridian points while speaking a "script." You can compose your own script once you learn the steps, or you can find Tapping videos and repeat the script in the video. When I began, I found videos I liked and repeated the script in the video. As I took more classes on Tapping, I began writing my own scripts for my meditations. Writing my own scripts was even more cathartic and enabled me to get in touch with my spirit on a deeper level.

Given the great success I was having with Tapping, I continued to take more spirituality classes that focused on meditation. While I absolutely adored Tapping and did it nearly every day, I was still looking for a meditation that was quieter and didn't require physical activity. I was still doing Transcendental meditation to fill this desire, but I knew that I needed to find something else.

In January of 2014, that something else came into my life with a bang. I signed up for a class that taught a specific type of guided meditation called the Silva Method. In the months leading up to this class, I had done other guided meditations, and they were a nice alternative to Transcendental meditation to do occasionally, but they were nothing to write home about. However, after the first time I did the Silva meditation, I felt a profound centeredness, deep connection with the Divine, and a relaxation in my body on a new level. It was quite simply an experience that I had never had before. I didn't even know that I could go that deep. After my first experience with the Silva Method, it became my go-to practice. If I had time after I finished the Silva meditation, I would do Transcendental meditation for another 10 minutes or so.

I was so excited that I had finally discovered my trifecta of meditation techniques that worked for the current state of my muscle control. Not only did my new meditation regime feel good to my body, but I also noticed that things in my life started happening with greater ease.

I also began feeling just how much I missed my colleagues in the office. By the time I discovered the Silva Method, I had been working from home exclusively for about one full year. While I was still having great success professionally—I had been promoted, many public policy papers that I had co-authored were being published, and I was in high demand to work on various projects—I felt disconnected and isolated from my colleagues. When I was on phone calls with my colleagues, we would almost always take time to chat before discussing work, but this was my only social interaction with my co-workers.

Although I was aware that I missed seeing my colleagues before I began doing the Silva meditation, I didn't know of any actions I could take to remedy the situation. Going into the office was not healthy for me, and although

I had great professional relationships with my colleagues, we didn't socialize on the weekends or hang out together after work. Thus, I was at a loss as to how to create more opportunities to connect with my colleagues on a personal level. I wasn't comfortable sharing these feelings with my colleagues because I felt it wasn't appropriate or professional.

Two months after I incorporated the Silva Method into my meditation practice, I had a check-in meeting with my new supervisor, James, who had taken over Brian's supervisory responsibilities.

I enjoyed having Brian as my supervisor, so I was less than thrilled about the change when I first heard the news; however, James turned out to be a fantastic supervisor who was just as committed to supporting my professional growth and understanding of my disability-related access needs as Brian had been. During my check-in meeting with James in March 2014, the bulk of the conversation centered around discussing work items. Once we finished everything on James's agenda, we talked about the changes in the office that had taken place over the year I had been working from home exclusively.

"It sounds like a whole different place," I said as he filled me in.

"Yes. The number of staff and office footprint have grown."

As he continued to talk, I said, "I really miss seeing and talking to everyone in the office. It sounds like so much has happened."

Without missing a beat, James asked, "Allison, where do you live?"

"Right in Cambridge. Actually, I'm about a 15-minute drive from the office. Well, without traffic that is. With traffic, you might get here faster if you walk."

After laughing, James said, "Would you be comfortable if a few of us from the office came over one day to have lunch with you?"

"Yes! That would be great!" I said in complete disbelief. I was so excited that it took every ounce of determination I had not to scream out loud.

After giving James a few details about where I lived and its proximity to public transportation, we hung up and I proceeded to do a happy dance. I wasn't sure how many people would be able to come over or even when they would be able to come, as every employee had a busy workday, but just the thought that my supervisor would look into having a get-together in a manner that was acces-sible to me was enough for a celebration.

After a few weeks of e-mails between James and me to work out the logistics of our Mathematica shindig, the day of the lunch arrived. I was in the lobby of my apartment building chatting with a friend when I saw a large group of my colleagues come in the main entrance of my apartment building.

"Hi, everyone!" I said, not even trying to hide my excitement.

"Hi, Allison! It's great to see you," James said as he walked up the steps.

Earlier in the week, the manager of my apartment building agreed to arrange the furniture in the clubhouse for my colleagues and I to have lunch together, and as we approached, I saw that the room was perfectly arranged for a lunch for 12 people with a large table surrounded by chairs.

As everyone got their food, drink, and cutlery, the talking, laughing, and camaraderie flowed. Although I had not seen any of my colleagues in over a year, it felt like I had just seen them yesterday. We talked about everything from work to movies to family as we ate delicious wraps and salads. I had so much fun talking and laughing with everyone face-to-face and feeling the vibe that initially attracted me to Mathematica. As the meal wound down and people needed to get back to the office, everyone said that they would like to do this again.

"I'd love that! This was so much fun, and it was great to see everyone again," I said.

"Okay. We'll definitely plan something," James said.

During the meal, I was listening to one person recount a story. As I listened, I realized just how much I missed this and what an amazing company I worked for. After everyone else left, James stayed so that we could do my annual performance review. Once the review was completed, I thanked James for everything he did to arrange the get-together. I understood the time, effort, and resources it took for him to arrange the lunch, and I wanted to make sure he knew that I appreciated it. However, it wasn't until a few months later that I realized the role that my new meditation practice had played in helping to manifest the community and connection that I desired.

For so long, Transcendental meditation enabled me to manifest the desires of my heart, because I was able to soak in my oneness with the Divine while meditating. However, once my muscle control began to change, the effectiveness of Transcendental meditation in helping me embody my connection with the Divine waned. This embodiment is the genesis of the manifestation of your authentic desires. When you embody the Divine, you embody your authentic desires. Over time, you surrender whatever mindset and perceptions that are holding you back from experiencing what you authentically desire, and you become the essence of that which you desire.

My new Silva and Tapping meditation practices allowed me to become the essence of community and connection. How was I community and connection? By having the courage to speak my authentic truth and ask for what I truly needed. God, the Divine, love itself is authenticity, truth, and courage. Prior to engaging in a meditation practice that met my current physical needs, I was too scared to speak my authentic truth. Concerns about how my colleagues would perceive me if I told them I missed seeing and connecting with them were at the forefront of my mind, rather than being true to myself and speaking authentically.

However, once I fully embodied my oneness with the Divine by meditating in a way that honored my body, I couldn't help but to be authentic and courageous. The words, "I miss everyone," just flowed out of my mouth without a moment's thought, because my meditation practice allowed me to quiet my ego mind and fearful thoughts and pour forth my divinity in the form of speaking my truth.

The ability to socialize with my colleagues in a manner that was healthy for me was a huge milestone and reflected my increasing openness due to meditation, but little did I know that an even more profound shift was underway.

I continued my meditation practice throughout the rest of 2014. However, the improvements in my health stopped. In fact, my health began to worsen again, as did my muscle control. To say that I was completely, beyond a shadow of a doubt, confused as to what my body needed to be healthy and to have the muscle control that I was accustomed to would have been the understatement of the millennium! I thought I had solved the question of my body with this work-from-home schedule and meditation practice, and yet, throughout 2014, my body showed me in every way possible that I had actually figured out very little. My health became increasingly precarious throughout the year.

So much so that 2014 culminated with me experiencing a serious bout of pneumonia soon after my three-year anniversary working at Mathematica. Since I have asthma, my respiratory system is compromised even when I'm completely healthy, so the last thing my respiratory system wanted to deal with was pneumonia! Pneumonia is serious for anyone, but for someone with CP, pneumonia carries with it an increased likelihood of death compared to those without CP.[2] In short, I was in a battle for my life. Thank goodness I had a wonderful support system and was able to successfully navigate through the illness.

Once I was through the most serious part of the illness, I knew I was officially at a very real fork in my road. Realizing that my life would be in jeopardy if I continued along the same path, I resigned from my position at Mathematica and put all of my time, energy, and attention into figuring out just what my body needed. In addition to going to doctors' appointments, researching physicians who specialized in treating adults with cerebral palsy, and seeking out nontraditional treatments, I also began to meditate for longer periods of time.

Since I was no longer working, I no longer had to make my meditation practice fit around my work schedule. Instead, I could meditate off and on throughout the day every day. When I worked, I'd meditate for about 30 minutes each evening on weekdays and for about an hour or so on the weekends. However, once I resigned, I meditated every day for about two hours working through the three types of meditation I had been doing for a couple of years by this point. But now, I did each meditation two times per day.

After two or three months of meditating for two hours every day, I began to realize something. For so long, my focus had been on getting my muscle control and health back to what it had been when I was around 20 years old, which is fine, but I wanted to achieve that goal with the same level of help I had always had. You see, since I was born with a disability, I spent a lot of my childhood working on being as independent and gaining as many physical skills as possible. By the time I enrolled in college as an 18-year-old, I was quite proud of all that I could do for myself physically. Although I still needed some assistance with certain tasks, I considered myself independent. My definition of independence remained the same from the time I was 18 years old until my 30s. However, after I began meditating more each day, I began to realize that my knowledge had expanded during those years, due to my formal education and simply living life. Thus, perhaps the time had come for me to expand my definition of what it meant for me to be independent.

Growing up, I was immersed in disability culture. One of the tenets of disability culture is that independence for disabled people doesn't require you to be able to physically do everything for yourself. Independence means that, regardless of what you are physically able to do, you have the support you need to live a self-determined life. Although I had taken that tenet to heart throughout my childhood and young adulthood in such a way that I knew I was independent even though I needed a bit of help, I began to realize that I could still be independent even if I allowed myself to receive more, much more, physical assistance. This was a radical concept for me and required a lot of soul searching and journaling to fully accept.

Although my increased time in daily meditation had led to this revelation, I still needed time to assimilate the revelation into my way of thinking. As I worked to become comfortable with this revelation, I continued to meditate two hours per day and had another revelation. Just as my mental abilities had changed over the time between college and working at Mathematica, it was okay if my physical abilities changed too. I realized that expecting my body to remain the same over 15 years was a bit of a stretch. I had never met someone, disabled or nondisabled, who said that their bodies were exactly the same as they had been 15 years earlier. Perhaps expecting my body to remain unchanged was, well, unrealistic.

Now I had two major shifts in my mindset to ease into. At this point, I was tempted to say, "Okay, God, we need to chat for a sec. I appreciate this expansion in my thinking, but I really need a moment to sit with all of this. My head is spinning so much from all of these discoveries that it's about to spin right into space. Can we please slow down all of these epiphanies?" But I didn't. I wanted to get my body to its optimal level of health and muscle control as soon as possible. So, I kept on meditating for two hours per day as my understanding of myself continued to evolve.

Just two weeks later, I had yet another epiphany. In all of my researching to figure out what my body needed, I was looking for the answer myself. I figured I was the expert on my body, hence I could figure out what it needed myself. While I was the expert on my body and the type of equipment it needed to remain healthy based on its abilities and needs when I was 20 years old, I had to admit to myself that although I was still the expert on my body, I did not know what equipment it needed now to be healthy. I realized that I needed to open myself up to receive guidance and suggestions from people who had more in-depth knowledge of disability-related equipment.

This epiphany was perhaps the hardest one to accept. To me, it meant relinquishing control and hoping that someone else knew what I needed when I didn't. This very concept flew in the face of just about everything I believed about my body. Up until that point, I felt I was the expert on me. That I just needed to put my mind to work, and I'd be able to figure out what was needed. For so long, almost my whole life in fact, I knew exactly what I needed, and how I needed it. But now, so many of the things that had helped my body be healthy and mobile were no longer effective.

For example, up until my early 30s, if I began having more difficulty than normal keeping my balance when I was standing, I knew that I needed to do more of a certain exercise. However, midway through my time at Mathematica, if I did more repetitions of that specific exercise, my balance got worse, not better. And other exercises that had helped me stay strong in my teens and 20s now caused my muscles to spasm and cramp uncontrollably. Instead of my exercises helping my muscles, they seemed to only exacerbate the decreasing muscle control.

In light of what was going on with my body, my epiphany showed me that continuing to expect myself to figure out what to do without any outside input was antithetical to me reaching my goals, because I was cutting myself off from receiving the help, support, and brilliance of those around me. By seeking to figure out everything on my own, I was stifling the flow of love, the flow of support, the flow of the Divine that surrounded me. Just as I felt called by the Divine to improve society through advocacy and economics, there were others who felt called to improve society by helping individuals with disabilities learn about and utilize pieces of equipment that could drastically improve their lives. Furthermore, collaborating with these people to manifest the environment and lifestyle that would enable me to live the life of my dreams was perfectly okay. I didn't have to do it all myself. God is in collaboration. So, I could collaborate.

By the time my third epiphany came, I felt like a completely different person. Even though my external environment looked the same, I had gone through a profound internal transformation. However, soon after my third epiphany, things in my external environment began to change too.

The first change occurred while I was writing my blog during the summer of 2015. While I loved blogging, the actual typing required to blog was quite painful for my hands, wrists, arms, neck, and shoulders, and breathing was becoming increasingly difficult for me whenever I typed. I used a laptop to type and typed with one finger on my right hand. While this had been the way I typed for most of my life, my current muscle control made pressing each button on the keyboard harder, which meant typing required more concentration. The increased concentration required to type caused breathing to become harder anytime I typed. Hence, typing using my finger became a Herculean task that felt like I was climbing Mount Everest backward and barefooted.

I knew I couldn't keep typing in this manner, so I decided to contact Tobii Dynavox, a company that creates, manufactures, and sells many devices that help people with disabilities live as independently as possible. I first heard about the company during my last year of graduate school when I was trying to determine the best computer setup for working at Mathematica. I met with an assistive technology specialist who recommended I try Tobii Dynavox's eyegaze attachment that would turn almost any computer into a computer that can be controlled with a person's eye movements. I tried the technology and loved it! Mathematica installed the attachment and software on my work computer. The eyegaze attachment allowed me to work easier and more efficiently. So, I reasoned that same technology would do the trick now.

I scheduled an appointment for a representative, Ben, from Tobii Dynavox to come to my home to make sure that the attachment would work on my laptop. Once Ben arrived at my home, he assessed my current computer, asked a few questions about my physical needs, and said, "Yes, this controller is compatible with your current laptop, but it seems to me that since there are times when you can't speak, you need a device that can also help you communicate."

"Oh. That would be great, but I still need something that I can use to navigate my computer," I said.

"Tobii has a device that speaks what you type into it and has additional functionality such as being a full computer and being able to control your thermostat and turn your lamps on and off. And you can control the entire device with your eye movements."

That sounded heavenly to me, so I tried the device and absolutely loved it. This device was even easier to control than the eyegaze attachment I had used for work. My caregivers also enjoyed the device because now I could simply type out my needs when I couldn't speak, instead of them having to ask me yes-no questions until they figured out what I needed. I had no idea that this device existed prior to my meeting with Ben, but with my willingness to collaborate with him and his expertise in eyegaze devices, I was able to manifest the perfect device for my current needs.

After demoing the device, I knew I wanted it. However, to receive this device, my doctor had to write a letter explaining why I needed it. So I called my doctor to explain the situation. She quickly understood that this device would be ideal for me and agreed to write the letter. After discussing this, she and I discussed my overall health. I told her that once I had a caregiver who could drive me places, I'd like to have physical therapy and occupational therapy. This led to the second change.

My doctor said, "You don't have to wait until you have transportation. With your current health insurance, I can arrange for you to receive in-home therapy visits."

You could have colored me shocked! I had gone to physical therapy (PT) and occupational therapy (OT) on and off from the time I was diagnosed with CP, but I never had someone offer to arrange for me to receive those therapies in my home. I always had those therapies at school or at a rehabilitation center. However, I was no longer in school and finding wheelchair-accessible transportation that could accommodate my respiratory needs was incredibly challenging, so getting to a rehabilitation center was far from easy. Thus, I eagerly agreed to having in-home therapy. Just a few days later, I began my therapies.

What I thought would be routine visits with a physical therapist and an occupational therapist to improve my flexibility, strength, and stamina turned out to be so much more. In addition to the exercises they did with me, each therapist also assessed my home and how I functioned in my home.

By my third PT and OT sessions, both therapists suggested pieces of equipment that would make my life easier and safer. My occupational therapist was less than impressed when she saw that I had to take a step into the shower and sit on a bench that provided no upper body support once I was in the shower. While this shower design was okay for me when I was in college, it was not safe for me now. Knowing that I needed full back support and head support when we did my exercises and in my daily activities, my occupational therapist strongly encouraged me to design my shower to give me the same level of support that my everyday wheelchair provided me with. While I knew that there were bath chairs that provided people with a lot of support, I had never seen a shower chair that provided that much support.

When I told my therapist this, she said, "That's why I'm here. To show you what's out there that might work better for you." We combed through every catalogue she had and found the perfect shower chair that not only provided support everywhere I needed it but was also on wheels, so I no longer had to step into and out of the shower.

My physical therapist was concerned that the bed I was sleeping in was not very supportive, was putting me in a position that was not ideal for my breathing, and was quite hard for me to get into and out of. In fact, when I showed her how I transferred from my wheelchair to my bed, she stopped me midway and said, "I've seen enough. We're getting you an adjustable bed with bed rails!"

Once I slept in my new bed for the first time and took my first shower in my brand-new shower chair, I wondered how on God's beautiful green Earth I had made it this long without this equipment! They made a huge difference in my life from the first moment I used them. Getting into and out of bed no longer felt like I was trying to balance on a tight rope. And once I was in bed, I could adjust my upper body and legs into any position so the constant involuntary movements that I experienced when I laid flat in my old bed were greatly diminished. I was also so much more comfortable, which made sleeping and breathing infinitely easier.

The impact of my shower chair was equally astounding. I no longer held on to the grab bars in my shower for dear life during my showers. Instead, I leaned back and relaxed in my tilting shower chair as the warm water flowed out of the nozzle. Showers were no longer stressful and scary—they became as enjoyable as they were when I was in college.

When I received my Tobii device and I could finally communicate effectively and easily any time, day or night, and I could type my blog posts without pain while breathing easily, I knew I was officially in heaven! In metaphysics, heaven is not a place you go to when you die. Heaven is a state of ever-unfolding good that you can experience anytime you are in complete alignment with the Divine. Due to the increased time I spent meditating, I had so aligned myself with the Divine that I was definitely in that state with all of my equipment and my team of incredible therapists who were dedicated to my well-being.

In addition to being able to communicate better and easier, the arrival of Tobii in my life meant I could also do Internet research much more efficiently and effectively. So, when I was not busy using Tobii to chat or blog, I used Tobii to research doctors who specialized in treating adults with cerebral palsy. While many, and I do mean many, physicians specialize in treating children with cerebral palsy, very few physicians treat adults with CP. This means that many adults with CP do not receive appropriate care and don't know what equipment, services, and medications exist that can help them live their best lives. I began looking for a physiatrist, which is the official name for doctors who treat adults with CP, over a year earlier . . . to no avail.

However, with Tobii by my side (and literally in front of me), I searched like nobody's business and finally found one physiatrist near my home. I immediately made an appointment to see him. While I waited for my appointment day to arrive, I typed out a document that detailed the changes in my muscle control. Once I began typing out everything, I realized that the changes began slowly when I was in college and had just picked up steam as the years progressed.

The day of my appointment I was so excited that I felt like I was levitating. I almost felt that I didn't need my wheelchair to get to his office. I could've simply floated right through the door, but gravity being gravity, I went ahead and used my wheelchair. Once he introduced himself and I got settled in his office, I handed him the document I had typed up, and within five minutes of meeting me, he knew exactly the type of CP I had, the events of my birth that caused the CP, and based on the type of CP I had, my educational level. To say I was astounded would have been like saying the Atlantic Ocean is just a mere puddle of water! I was beyond amazed to be meeting with a physician who knew so much about CP. We talked about my overall muscle control, and after moving my limbs, he explained that I actually have two types of CP, not just one. Until that point, I had always been told that I had one type of CP. However, I had always wondered why my muscle control was different in different parts of my body.

We then turned to my document. He asked a few clarifying questions as he read, made several notes, and once he finished, he said, "We've got some work to do. The good news is everything you've been experiencing is common for adults with CP."

"It is? That would've been helpful to know 10 years ago. I thought I was doing something wrong."

"No, you haven't done anything wrong. What you're experiencing is called aging with CP."

Once he finished his statement, I couldn't help but think, "'Aging with CP'? Really? They couldn't have given it a more upbeat or jazzier name? I could've thought of at least 50 names better than that, but alas, I am at this appointment to help my body, not rename a condition . . . no matter how much it is in need of rebranding."

I must have made a face that matched my thoughts, because the doctor said, "I know you're only in your 30s, so it might be weird to think about aging. But CP puts a significant strain on the body, which causes adults with CP to experience changes in their physical functioning as early as their late teens. Just like CP, aging with CP can cause different symptoms for each person. For you, we'll most likely do a combination of medication, the addition of new services, and perhaps surgery."

From there, the doctor and I developed a plan of action that made a difference within hours. Yes, you read that correctly: hours!

Amid all the additions and changes in my home and lifestyle that made my life easier throughout the autumn of 2015 and the beginning of 2016, the year 2015 ended with me receiving equipment that literally saved my life. Throughout my time working at Mathematica and after I resigned, my muscle control changed so that speaking, standing, sitting, walking, breathing, holding my head up, and using my hands all became increasingly difficult. During that time, I noticed another change that was a bit more serious. I started choking whenever I ate.

When I was a little girl, my parents always cut up my food into small bite-sized pieces, made sure that anything I ate was tender so I could chew it with ease, and insisted that I always sat with proper back support whenever I ate. With these precautions, eating was always a breeze. It took longer for me to eat my meals because of the time it took for me to coordinate my oral muscles. However, other than needing extra time to eat and utilizing the same precautions I used when I was little, I never gave eating a second thought, until the beginning of my second year of working. I noticed that I was choking a few times during every dinner. This was odd because I was eating the way I always had, but now the food seemed to be going down the wrong way pretty routinely. I figured I was just fatigued and once I caught up on my rest, I would stop choking.

However, this did not happen. Although I was working from home exclusively and resting more, over the next year and a half, the choking grew worse instead of better. My caregivers and I thought perhaps I needed my food cut into smaller pieces. So they began chopping up my food in a food processor, which made chewing so much easier, and voilà . . . the choking I had been experiencing vanished! However, after about a year of chopping my food up in a food processor, the choking came roaring back, and I was at a loss as to what to do. So I asked my mother for advice. She suggested making my food into a pureed consistency.

Eating food with a pureed texture worked brilliantly until the autumn of 2014. At this time, I began choking again. Through the end of 2014 and all of 2015, the choking grew worse and more intense. By the fall of 2015, I was choking on every single bite I took—breakfast, lunch, dinner, snacks. You name it, I choked on it. It seemed like all I had to do was merely look at food, and I began choking. Generally, by the end of every meal, I'd be drenched in sweat, exhausted, out of breath, and my voice would be hoarse from all of the coughing and gagging I did while eating. I had always been a foodie and loved to eat, but now eating had become a less-than-fun chore that I had to complete several times every day. With all of the choking I did during every meal, eating became quite physically demanding. The sheer physicality of eating resulted in me burning more calories than I consumed whenever I ate. So, by the autumn of 2015, I was significantly underweight.

A member of my health care team was concerned about my weight and referred me to a nutritionist. The nutritionist made an appointment to see me one night while I ate dinner. Upon seeing the amount of food that was on my plate for dinner, she said, "Do you usually eat this much?"

"Oh yeah. Because of the CP, I have to eat a ton of calories to keep my weight up," I replied.

She said, "Okay." However, I could tell she was trying to figure out how I could eat so much and be underweight. I proceeded to eat, and choke, for about five minutes.

In between bites, she asked if every meal was like this. Since I was out of breath from coughing, my caregiver answered, "Every single meal is like this."

She observed me take a few more bites and then said, "Allison, I'm going to leave now. You need to concentrate on eating, and I don't want to interfere with that. I'll be in touch tomorrow. Okay?"

The next day, I received a call from a speech-language pathologist (SLP) who said that I had been referred to her for swallowing difficulties. After an initial consultation with the SLP in which she observed me eat dinner, the SLP arranged for me to have a swallowing test done as soon as possible.

After three years of trying to figure out what was going on with my eating ability and losing a significant amount of weight, over the course of a 10-minute test I finally received an answer. I had something called dysphagia, which is the medical term for difficulty swallowing. The test revealed that I had a severe form of it. The usual course of action was to try foods with different textures to see if the person can swallow certain textures better than others. Since I was choking quite severely on purées, the only other texture I could try was a thickened liquid texture . . . I choked on that too.

The SLP and nutritionist scheduled a time to see me, together. I knew that if they wanted to see me at the same time, I was in for a doozy of an appointment. I was right. As it turned out, they suggested that I get a feeding tube, technically called a gastrostomy tube (or g-tube), and receive all of my nutrition, hydration, and medication through the tube. I wasn't completely surprised by the news and was beyond relieved that I finally had a game plan that would make eating easier. However, this would be a huge change and a serious step into the unknown, so I needed a moment to take it all in. I asked for a hug, which they were happy to provide, and then we figured out all the details.

Just over a week later, I had surgery and officially became a tubie, which is what people who use feeding tubes call themselves.

I spent the first week after surgery in the hospital recovering and receiving pain medication so I could rest as much as possible. My mom, who had flown into town to be with me after the surgery, and caregivers took turns staying with me. Once I was deemed ready to be released, I went home to continue recuperating. My parents and sister each took turns staying with me the first two weeks I was home. Over the course of the three weeks after surgery, I steadily gained weight and gradually spent more time awake as the pain from the procedure subsided and my body adjusted to my feeding tube. While I would sit in my wheelchair for a few minutes here and there, I spent most of those weeks in bed, letting the incision heal.

However, by the beginning of the fourth week after my surgery, I felt something odd . . . energy! I had so much energy, I didn't know what to do with myself. My caregiver helped me get into my wheelchair that day, and I was able to sit up in my chair *all day*! It had been a few years since I had been strong enough to sit up for more than a couple of hours at a time. As the days went on, I felt more and more incredible! I spoke to my mom on the phone one day and said, "Mom, I feel so amazing now! I didn't even realize how not well I felt for so long until now, because now I feel amazing!"

As my energy level continued to increase and my stamina improved, I felt more and more gratitude toward my feeding tube, feeding pump, and formula. It was remarkable to experience what a difference the proper equipment can make in one's life.

To this day, I am still beyond grateful to the feeding tube, who I affectionately call Twila, the feeding pump, and the formula that enable me to be healthy, active, and alive. Twila not only saved my life, but she gave me my life back! Now, don't get me wrong. Life with a feeding tube is vastly different than life without being hooked up to life support and requires a completely different lifestyle. But I welcome that lifestyle with open arms and an open heart.

I often tell people that Twila saved my life, but the truth is that meditation saved me. Through meditation, I incrementally expanded my consciousness to be receptive to receiving help—life-saving help—in any form. I released notions about independence and what my body "should" be capable of doing. Once I had surrendered those beliefs and thought patterns that no longer served me, the Divine presence within me shined through and radiated throughout my life. Since my divinity was able to shine unencumbered, I was fully aligned with love, openness, possibility, intelligence, and ingenuity. In fact, because I was aligned with those qualities, I embodied those qualities. I was the very essence of what I needed to be in order to save my body.

When I began meditating two hours per day, I didn't say to myself, "Self, I need to change my beliefs about these three things, thus I'm going to meditate. So, meditation, do your thing." At the time, I was completely unaware that these thoughts were even part of my consciousness. The thoughts had become so ingrained in my mindset that they were just present in my energy and part of the way I lived my life. However, they formed the lens through which I viewed, and experienced, the world. I didn't even realize the lens was there until my meditation practice revealed to me in fluorescent, neon flashing lights that I had these beliefs.

This is one of the many gifts of meditation. You don't need to know what thought patterns need to be released in order for meditation to help you transmute them. By the grace of God, when you meditate as much as is healthy for you in a way that honors your body and mind, the beliefs that you hold that are not serving your best interests will simply come into your awareness for you to release.

In *A Course in Miracles*, we are taught that God can only do for us what It can do through us.[3] I understand this to mean that a miraculous life filled with joy, love, peace, and so many other Divine qualities are ours for the living *if* we are willing to embody these qualities by *being* joyful, loving, and peaceful. How do you embody these, or any other, Divine qualities you wish? By engaging in spiritual practice, by choosing to know that you are Divine, and by choosing to cultivate these qualities within yourself.

Meditation enables us to cultivate Divine qualities within ourselves by allowing us to focus on our oneness with God without any distractions. Cultivating Divine qualities within ourselves through meditation proceeds in three stages: release, clearing, and evolution.

In the first stage, we release beliefs, perspectives, and opinions that we have acquired throughout our lives that are out of alignment with God. When we are born, we come from the realm of the Divine onto planet Earth. We come into this world without opinions, attitudes, and a belief system about the world. Instead, we come into this world in the full awareness of our oneness with God. After all, how many six-month-olds have you met with a fully formed belief system about money, or romantic relationships, or our political system? I have met exactly zero infants who have an opinion about any of those things. However, as we grow up and live our lives, we are taught beliefs, opinions, and perspectives about the world by our families, our culture, and social norms.

These beliefs and opinions form our experiences. Have you ever heard the saying, "If you think you live in a friendly universe, you're right, and if you think you live in an unfriendly universe, you're right"? This saying speaks to the fact that our beliefs shape our lives because we perceive what we believe. This is because when our conscious mind is interested in something, our subconscious mind does everything it can to bring our attention to anything that is related, or supports the activity of our conscious mind. Have you ever asked a friend to pick you up in a public place and the friend agreed and told you to look for the green car that he'd be driving? And all you saw for the week after your friend picked you up was green cars? This is your subconscious bringing your attention to what your conscious mind is interested in.

As Neville Goddard writes in *Feeling Is the Secret,*

> *The conscious generates ideas and impresses these ideas on the subconscious; the subconscious receives ideas and gives form and expression to them. The subconscious does not originate ideas, but accepts as true those which the conscious mind feels to be true. The subconscious never alters the accepted beliefs of man. It out-pictures them to the last detail whether or not they are beneficial. The subconscious is the womb of creation. . . It never changes the idea received, but always gives it form.*[4]

The same phenomenon is at work in each and every belief system. You will experience the evidence of whatever position you choose to adopt. Thus, our experiences are directly influenced by our beliefs, opinions, perceptions, and perspectives of the world. Often, we are not directly experiencing the world around us; we are experiencing our opinions, thoughts, and perspectives *about* the world around us. This experience can be so positive and healthy if our opinions, beliefs, and perspectives emanate from our oneness with the Universal Presence, emphasizing the joy, wonder, and interconnectedness of the Universe, but because many of the beliefs and perspectives that we learn throughout our lives are not based in the truth of God, they cause us to have painful experiences. These negative beliefs range from self-doubt and fear of change all the way to bigotry and hate. When we go into meditation, we are working to dissolve the beliefs and perspectives that we have picked up in our daily lives that are not the truth of the Divine.

This dissolution happens because, as we meditate, we cease thinking incessantly about the matters of the material world, and instead do our best to focus on our oneness with the Divine, by focusing on a mantra, focusing on our breath, or focusing on the words of a guided meditation. This intentional, conscious focus inward is stage one of your meditation practice, and however an individual chooses to begin—silently seated on a cushion in lotus position or listening to a favorite meditation app sprawled on their bed—the results are the same. By removing our attention from the matters of the world and focusing on our oneness with God, we are separating ourselves from our past experiences and reacquainting ourselves with the Divine, with the place from which we came, with the knowledge of our true selves. Each time we meditate, we are interrupting the patterns found in the human mind and are supplanting those patterns with the qualities of God.

As you focus on your breath, or your mantra, or the words of a guided meditation, you will enter into the second stage of meditation: clearing. During this phase, your body might feel fidgety or itchy, or your mind may have thoughts racing through it, or you may experience strong emotions. I know this sounds far from enticing and you might be thinking, "And just why would I voluntarily do this to myself?" The discomfort of this phase is often the block that causes many to think they can't meditate or it's too hard for them, after all. But the reason it's important to embrace this struggle and do the work here is that in order to get to the desired result of embodiment and living from a place of oneness with the Divine Creator, we must release all of the "stuff" that we have picked up since our birth. Some of that stuff—even the worst, most hurtful beliefs we carry—can feel natural and safe since we have carried it for so long. This process is like the realization you are wearing a heavy suit of armor that you put on to fight a battle years ago, but now it is weighing you down as you try to move through life and relationships wearing it. This armor is burdening you, keeping others away, and hurting you more than it's protecting you.

In meditation, we are focused on our oneness with God, so anything that is out of alignment with that oneness will come to the forefront of our awareness so that it can be purged or transmuted into a quality of God, such as love, joy, generosity, or freedom. You can take away your armor of protection, for example, and surround yourself instead with the protective loving embrace of your loved ones and community. All we need to do to complete the clearing process is continue to meditate and consciously commit to growth and evolution. As our thoughts, opinions, and perspectives clear, we release those qualities within ourselves that limit our understanding of God, bringing us closer to our oneness with God. The releasing of the opinions and perspectives accumulated from the world causes the qualities of God—love, joy, abundance, intelligence, generosity, and so many others—to become increasingly active in our thoughts, feelings, and behavior and in the external circumstances of our lives.

As we release those perspectives that we picked up during our lifetime on this Earth, we also open ourselves up to the Divine to speak to us via intuition or an epiphany or a new perspective. During this third stage, we suddenly or incrementally come to know spiritual truths, such as God is everywhere, or we are one with God. As we continue to meditate, these realizations become anchored within us, and we begin to feel differently, think differently, and behave differently. Regular meditation causes our perceptions and opinions about the world to change, and ultimately our reality and experience of the world changes too.

While the act of meditating is important to our experiencing a life of love, joy, and abundance, the amount of time we spend in meditation during each session and the frequency of our meditation sessions are just as important. The more time we spend in meditation during each session and the more consistently we meditate, the more deeply we align our human mind and emotions with the Divine. The more time we spend with God in meditation, the more we embody the qualities of God such as generosity, kindness, wisdom, and a loving nature. The more deeply we allow these qualities to penetrate our mindsets, personalities, and decision-making, the more we embody the Divine and the easier life flows. We show up differently and life shows up differently for us.

The more I meditated, the more I embodied the Divine, which caused me to *be* the love and joy that I sought to experience in the world around me and to *bring* that love and joy with me wherever I went. One of the beautiful aspects of spiritual practices is that all you need is a sincere desire to be a source of light in the world and to commit to your practice to reap its benefits.

By cultivating our connection through meditation, we live increasingly in the miraculous grace of God, which manifests itself as life flowing smoothly and overflowing with love, joy, and God's goodness.

HOW TO MEDITATE

Exercises and Prompts

There are so many types of meditation: active meditation, body scan meditation, guided meditation, Transcendental meditation, movement meditation, contemplative meditation, etc.—all beneficial and valid ways to approach this spiritual practice. I encourage you to do an Internet search of the other types of meditation listed and try them out to see if another type of meditation is better for you. This section focuses on the type of meditation that I personally work with most in my life: Transcendental meditation.

Exercise 1: Build a Transcendental meditation practice.

1. *Set up your environment.* Before beginning your meditation session, find a quiet place in your home or outside. Get comfortable with blankets, pillows, cozy clothes, and loose hair so you aren't distracted by the space around you.
2. *Position your body.* Sit in an arrangement that lends itself to you remaining awake during the session. Most meditation teachers suggest sitting in a chair or on the floor

cross-legged, but choose the position that is most comfortable for you. If you need to be in a reclined position in your bed or wheelchair, meditating in a reclined position works as well. I often meditate in a reclined position in my bed to reduce the involuntary movements in my arms and legs.

3. *Set a timer.* Choose how long you would like to spend in meditation and set a timer. This helps you to go deeper into meditation without worrying about checking the clock again and again. If you are beginning a new meditation practice, start meditating for two-minute sessions to get your body used to the practice.
4. *Be gentle with yourself.* You might feel fidgety or have thoughts racing through your mind as you start or when you experience strong emotions. This is normal, and it occurs as part of the "purging process" of meditation. Be gentle with yourself and persist through this discomfort. Meditation is a practice, so the more you do it, the more comfortable it becomes. Once you have been able to meditate for two minutes per day for seven days comfortably, try meditating for five minutes each session. Once you have meditated for five minutes each session for 10 days, try meditating for 10 minutes each session.
5. *Choose your mantra.* Transcendental meditation requires us to close our eyes, choose a mantra,

and say the mantra in our minds each time we inhale and each time we exhale for the entire meditation session. A mantra is a word or phrase that you choose to focus on. Some people choose a one-word mantra that describes a quality of God that they want to experience more of like: love, harmony, peace, abundance, joy, or bliss. Others choose mantras that are phrases that focus on their breathing such as: "I am breathing in. I am breathing out," or "Breathing in now. Breathing out now." Play around with the mantras listed here and see if one feels particularly good to you.

6. *Don't worry if your mind wanders during the meditation.* As soon as you are aware that your mind has wandered, gently bring your attention back to your breathing and resume thinking your mantra with each inhale and exhale.
7. *Winding down.* Once you complete your meditation session, sit quietly for between 30 seconds and five minutes. When you meditate, you are doing a lot of inner work and rearranging your inner world. After doing such work, giving yourself time to acclimate to your new world by sitting quietly helps you to re-establish your balance and embody the changes you have just experienced.

ACCESS NOTES

Exercise 1: Build a Transcendental meditation practice.

1. *If you have Attention Deficit Hyperactivity Disorder (ADHD),* I'd suggest you try mindfulness meditation before Transcendental meditation. Studies have shown that this type of meditation works especially well for those with ADHD. In mindfulness meditation, you sit quietly, close your eyes, and focus on the sensation of your belly moving in and out as you breathe. If you become aware that you are thinking about something, bring your attention back to your breath and the sensation of your belly moving.

   When you begin your meditation practice, experts suggest sitting for five minutes per day for a two-week period. After two weeks, increase your sessions to six minutes. After another two weeks, increase to seven minutes and so on, until you reach the maximum amount of time you are able to meditate during each session. For some people the maximum amount of time of their meditation session is 10 minutes, for others the maximum is 25 minutes. You can determine your own sweet spot. If you're interested in learning more about mindfulness meditation for those with ADHD, consider reading the book *The Mindfulness Prescription for Adult ADHD* by Dr. Lidia Zylowska.

2. *If you use a ventilator to breathe,* you may wonder if focusing on your breath is as effective for connecting with the Divine as it is for those who do not require mechanical ventilation. The answer is *yes, absolutely*! God is everywhere, which means God is in the air that is propelled through your air hose into your lungs just as much as It is in the air that surrounds us. So yes, focusing on your breath, regardless of how oxygen enters your body, can lead to a greater awareness of your connection with God. The key is to determine if meditation is a practice that feels good to you.
3. *If you cannot feel air entering and exiting your nostrils or you cannot feel your belly move as you breathe,* you may find that focusing on a sound in your environment as you meditate helps you relax more than focusing on your breath.
4. *If you have involuntary movements,* it's okay if you move while meditating. Often, I see pictures and videos of people who are meditating, and they are completely still. My muscles don't stay still that long, and sometimes if I don't move for a prolonged period of time, my muscles cramp. So if you need to move while meditating, please feel free to do so and know that you are still aligning yourself with God. I recommend moving when movement will keep your body comfortable and healthy.
5. *If you have bipolar disorder with mania and symptoms of psychosis,* you should speak with your doctor before starting a meditation practice. Certain types of meditation are

associated with episodes of psychosis. So, if you are interested in practicing meditation, you should work with your treatment team to adapt meditation to fit your abilities.

6. *If you have addiction or a substance use disorder,* three types of meditation are especially effective. The first type is mindfulness meditation. See ACCESS NOTE 1 in this chapter for a description of this type of meditation. The second type is movement meditation. This type of meditation includes tai chi, yoga, or going for a walk in nature and focusing your mind on the sensations of your body as you walk. Gordon Goad[5], someone who provides assistance to those with substance use disorder, recommends the final type of meditation: water meditation. Water meditation involves the following steps:

   a. Run a warm bath.

   b. Light a scented candle and put it in your bathroom or add bath salts or oils to your bathwater.

   c. Once your bathtub is full, turn the tap so that small drips of warm water drip into the tub.

   d. Get comfortable in your bathtub.

   e. Concentrate on your breath. Inhale deeply and exhale slowly. Feel the air as it enters and exits your nose.

   f. If your mind gets distracted, focus on the sound of the dripping water.

CHAPTER SIX

gratitude

Gratitude is the highest form of prayer.[1]

—LOUIX DOR DEMPRIEY

You might be thinking to yourself, "Gratitude! How is gratitude a spiritual practice? That's just something we teach children so that they are polite." Or, you may have heard that you should keep a gratitude journal, but you are a bit fuzzy about why or how gratitude can help you live a better life. Let me de-fuzz you a bit.

We all have two minds: the conscious and the subconscious. The conscious mind is filled with our thoughts, opinions, likes, dislikes, etc. In short, it's our "thinking brain." We use it to make plans, think through options, and the like. It's quite proactive. Our conscious mind transmits signals and messages to our subconscious mind. The subconscious mind is active when we sleep and dream, among other times.

Many people believe they make things happen with their conscious minds. After all, that is the mind responsible for making plans and decisions. However, and this is a gargantuan however, the *subconscious* mind is responsible for creating the experiences we have in our lives. So the best way to create what you authentically desire is to align your subconscious with the Divine, and one way to do this is by feeling and expressing gratitude. When you express gratitude, your conscious mind is registering a simple "thank you" shared in conversation or written on a page, but you are also sending a signal to your subconscious mind that you have received something. Your subconscious mind absorbs that signal and creates circumstances in which you receive. The more gratitude you express, the more you fill your subconscious mind with abundance, love, joy, appreciation, and openness to receiving. Such a mind is in complete alignment with God, which causes blessings to pour upon you like a monsoon.

The extent to which you and God can co-create your authentic desires depends on the content of your subconscious. Is your subconscious filled with rancor and discontent? Or is your subconscious filled with happiness, love, and awe for the beauty of life? These are important questions because your subconscious is the soil in which you plant the seeds of your hopes and dreams. If that soil is lacking in nutrients, dry, and unbalanced, any seeds that you plant in it cannot flourish into the amazing opportunity you desire. You will never realize those dreams because the seeds of the dreams are not receiving the nourishment they need to come to fruition. If, however, your soil is rich and healthy—made of love, joy, and faith—any seeds planted in it have the best chance of taking root and bursting into bloom. Thus, the seeds of your dreams will grow into the fulfillment of your dreams. And because the seeds of your dreams are nourished by the qualities of God, the fulfillment of your dreams is enhanced by the loving energy of God. God's loving energy is the sun that shines down and the water that provides from below. Thus, not only do you grow a garden of your desires, but those experiences are more beautiful and God-filled than you could have imagined. It was by applying these principles that I found the perfect home for me at a time when I really needed it.

Midway through my last year of graduate school, my academic advisors had assured me that my dissertation would be approved for my Ph.D. degree, and I had already accepted a job offer. These two monumental events meant one thing: I was a few months away from graduating and moving into a new chapter of my life! Since I lived on campus during graduate school, my impending graduation also meant that I needed to find a wheelchair-accessible, three-bedroom apartment near my job. Given my generous salary, I thought that finding my first apartment would be easy. However—as almost anyone who has ever searched for accessible housing can attest—I was woefully mistaken.

After touring several apartment buildings in the area, I discovered two housing trends. First, the vast majority of wheelchair-accessible apartments available at market price had just one bedroom. Second, although an apartment may be advertised as "wheelchair accessible," it was most likely that it was accessible for someone using a manual wheelchair, not for someone using a motorized wheelchair or power wheelchair such as mine. Since manual wheelchairs tend to be smaller than power wheelchairs, an apartment that is accessible for a manual wheelchair user may not be accessible to a power wheelchair user simply because of the sheer size of power wheelchairs and the space they need to maneuver.

When I finally found an accessible two-bedroom apartment that could accommodate my power wheelchair in the same city as my job, I jumped at the opportunity to sign a lease. While the apartment didn't check all my boxes, the apartment building was gorgeous and filled with wonderful neighbors and staff and my apartment had magnificent views. Outside of my living room, home office, and two of my bedroom windows were views of rolling hills. These hills were covered with trees, and each evening the sun would set behind them, shining its last, brilliant rays and illuminating them from behind. It was absolutely gorgeous! Outside of the third window of my bedroom was a view of a tree-lined street with a few stores, which was perfect for people watching from the comfort of my bed.

Some people have asked me, "Allison, why was having a nice view so important? Sure, having beautiful views from your home is a nice bonus, but isn't that far from necessary?"

I can see why many people might think so. However, since I would be working from home two and a half days per week at a computer-oriented job, having beautiful surroundings to look at throughout the workday would support my creativity and give me much-needed rest periods from staring at the blaring white screen of my computer. Also, I adore being in nature, but going outside every day simply wouldn't be possible for me, due to cerebral palsy (CP).

I figured I could enjoy the great outdoors from the comfort of my home by living in an apartment with a front-row seat. Either way you look at it—to excel professionally and creatively or to accommodate my disability—I'm simply a woman meant to live in a home with gorgeous views.

For the first year or so I took in the beautiful views from my apartment's windows, and I relished each sunrise and sunset over the hills. And then it started to happen. Over the course of a couple of weeks, I started noticing a fleet of construction vehicles, construction workers milling around, and large holes appearing in the parking lots between my apartment building and the rolling hills in the distance. Curious about this unfolding scene, I took a stroll down the street and came upon a large metal fence encircling what was clearly a construction site. Above this fence was a sizable sign with a drawing of not one, not two, but three new apartment buildings that would be replacing all the parking lots.

I have a naturally sunny and optimistic disposition, so upon finding this sign, I was certain that I'd still have my glorious view of the rolling hills. I reasoned that these buildings could very well be shorter than the apartment building I lived in. Perhaps the new buildings would be wide but not tall. After all, there was so much land that surely the developers wouldn't build up, they'd just build wide. After this chat with myself, I happily drove my wheelchair back to my apartment.

Well, after several months of steady construction, the small holes in the former parking lots had become one gargantuan apartment building. I realized I had been partly correct: the new apartment building was quite wide. However, it was quite tall, as well. It was taller than my apartment building, which meant one-third of my view of the rolling hills was gone. I was less than thrilled by this, but I still hoped that maybe, just maybe, the other two new buildings would be shorter.

Nope! The other two buildings were just as tall as the first. So, in the span of approximately 18 months my view of the rolling hills became a wall of apartment buildings. On the upside though, the buildings were painted pretty colors. So, I did my best to enjoy looking at red, green, and blue facades. And the buildings were built far enough from mine so even though I no longer had a spectacular view, there was still open space surrounding my apartment building.

Around the same time that construction of the second building began, a new management company bought the apartment building that I lived in. While the new staff was friendly in person, my rent skyrocketed. My rent increased so much, so fast that I was pretty sure it was heading for the moon. Between my diminishing views and my stratospheric rent, even my sunny disposition was starting to cloud over. I tried to make the best of an untenable situation, but I knew that I had to move to a new home for my mental and financial health. Once I made the decision, I became quite excited for the move and began my search for a wheelchair-accessible, three-bedroom apartment within 30 minutes of the city in earnest.

I opened accounts on every apartment website I could find. I created alerts so I'd receive an e-mail when an apartment opened up in a building I liked. I was a woman on a mission.

My excitement waned a bit when I could find only seven wheelchair-accessible, three-bedroom apartments in the entire eastern part of my state, and they were all located at least one hour away from the city. There were slightly more two-bedroom accessible apartments, but I knew now from experience that I needed more space.

In the years since I had moved into this place, my CP symptoms had become more severe, which meant I now had more equipment to help me with my daily activities and I required more caregivers in my home to provide personal care and health services. With the increasing number of people and pieces of large equipment in my home, my apartment was bursting at the seams. I knew a two-bedroom apartment would not cut it anymore, but publicly listed three-bedroom apartments were nowhere to be found.

Given the lack of options, I thought the next logical step was contacting leasing offices to see if they had available apartments that were unlisted. Although I found a few promising apartments using this technique, the leasing office of every apartment building with whom I arranged a tour canceled my tour two days before the tour, saying that the apartment I was interested in had been rented. After the sixth cancellation, I decided to take a rest from the apartment hunting.

A few months into my apartment-hunting hiatus, I awoke to a familiar sound: jackhammering. Unlike the distant jackhammering I heard when the three apartment buildings were being built, this was incredibly loud. It sounded like someone was jackhammering next to my bedroom window that overlooked the beautiful tree-lined street. However, on that side of the building was a narrow service road, a set of train tracks, and a small patch of dirt. Since nothing could be built on the train tracks and surely an entire building could not be shoe-horned between the service road and my building where the patch of land resided, I asked my caregiver what she saw out there.

Knowing that I was still adjusting to my view of apartment buildings, she turned toward me and in a very gentle voice she said, "Allison, it looks like they're building something out there."

"No!" I cried out. Six weeks after the sound of jackhammering woke me up, my beautiful view of the tree-lined street had become a view of an eight-story, concrete, utilitarian parking garage that blocked 80 percent of the sun's light from entering my bedroom. The garage was so close to my building that I was certain that if I put my hand out of the window and really stretched, I could touch the cars parked in the garage. I had many feelings about this hulking piece of concrete that had obliterated my gorgeous view, but gratitude definitely was not one of them. I felt more disgust for the structure than anything else.

Now more than ever, I knew I had to move as soon as possible. So, I started looking for a new apartment . . . again. This time I redoubled my efforts by e-mailing more leasing agents, expanding the number of cities I was willing to move to, and even allowing myself to consider moving to a two-bedroom apartment for the time being. I simply knew that I could not continue living in an apartment where all I saw was concrete or the sides of other apartment buildings. The ability to enjoy nature and comfortably pay my rent were just too important to my mental health. However, the moving gods did not get the memo that I needed to move to a better location immediately, and I was starting to feel a bit stuck.

I hunted for my new home from early spring through the summer without success. Once autumn commenced, it was clear that I would be staying in my apartment for another winter. I live in New England, and while I absolutely loved skiing in winter as a kid, there was no way I was going to move during a New England winter. So, I prepared myself to stay put for at least six more months. As committed as I was to my spiritual practices, no breakthrough in my living arrangements was occurring.

During my hiatus from apartment hunting, I was in the midst of being assessed for more caregiver hours because I needed more assistance to sit in my wheelchair and engage in other activities; however, the increase in hours had not been approved by my insurance yet, which meant I was spending most of my time in bed. Since I'm a woman who loves to be on the go, spending lots of time in bed while I was completely healthy was not quite what I had envisioned for myself. But I decided early on that I needed to use this time to reflect on my spiritual practices and my living situation.

Throughout my apartment-hunting adventures, I engaged in my usual spiritual practices of meditation and prayer because I knew that all blessings, including the perfect home, flow from my oneness with God. However, my time in bed gave me time to think, and I realized that I needed to do something new. Since I wanted a home with amenities that I never had, I needed to engage in spirituality in new ways. Specifically, I needed to expand my understanding of spiritual principles and engage in a new spiritual practice, a spiritual practice that built upon my current practices but ushered me into greater alignment with God.

With these insights, I used my time in bed to read books on spirituality. One of the books I read is entitled *Ask and It Is Given* by Esther and Jerry Hicks. I also read the companion book, *The Processes*. While *Ask and It Is Given* teaches the spiritual principles behind receiving your desires, it also teaches spiritual practices, many of them unknown to me. I began working with all the practices described in the book, but one resonated with me so profoundly that it became the cornerstone of my daily spiritual practice. The Hickses call it the "Rampage of Appreciation."

The Rampage of Appreciation requires you to spend 10 minutes saying what you are grateful for. The most important part of this practice is that you feel immersed in gratitude for the entire 10 minutes. Since I have difficulty speaking for 10 consecutive minutes, I often did the Rampage by thinking about what I was grateful for.

Each time I completed the Rampage, I was on such a natural high and felt so much love, joy, and gratitude for all I had been given that I didn't want to stop. When I had the time and energy, I did the Rampage for 15 minutes. It was pure fun!

After about a week of doing the Rampage on a daily basis, I noticed something, well, a few things actually. Whenever I looked out of my window that overlooked the three apartment buildings, birds were hovering next to the window. I never noticed birds flitting about next to this window before, but now they seemed to be gathering there every day. I also started noticing more birds swooping in beautiful formations past my window. Dazzled by my numerous winged visitors, I spent an increasing amount of time looking up at the sky. I wanted to know what the birds were doing before they arrived at my window. As I spent more time looking at the sky, I witnessed more nature than I ever remember seeing before. I was noticing the absolutely gorgeous colors of the sky and all the cool shapes of the clouds. I was falling in love with the view of nature that I *did* have instead of obsessing about the one I didn't.

The longer I did the Rampage, the more beauty I saw outside my window and the more grateful I became for my awesome home with the amazing view. My gratitude grew organically. As my gratitude expanded, my awareness of the less-than-ideal parking garage shrank. In fact, after a few weeks of looking only at the sky, I completely forgot about the garage and apartment buildings!

I didn't realize how much my perspective about my home had changed until the beginning of spring when a fill-in caregiver was covering for one of my regular caregivers. After opening the blinds in my living room, she said "What a terrible view! You used to have such a nice view, but now all you see are buildings!"

I looked out of the window that she was standing in front of, and without a thought, I said, "You know, I don't even see the buildings anymore. I sit reclined in my bed so much now that all I see is the pretty sky, birds, and an occasional airplane."

My words shocked me. For a minute, I didn't think I had actually said them. How in the world did I go from being disillusioned by the view outside my window to absolutely loving the view?

A Course in Miracles teaches that a miracle is a change in one's perspective. When you change your perspective, you quite literally change your world. By choosing to focus on the nature I could see outside my window from the new perspective of my bed, I experienced a miracle. I went from seeing a world of concrete and metal to seeing a world of open sky filled with beauty, joy, and freedom. I hadn't realized what a profound shift had taken place in my mind until that moment. And I was so proud of myself that I did a little dance right there—change had come, just not in the way I had originally expected.

A few weeks later, I redoubled my efforts to look for a new home. After perusing various websites, I found several apartment buildings that I liked and began e-mailing leasing agents to schedule tours. I began my first e-mail with my usual question—did the building have accessible three-bedroom apartments available—but an inspired thought came to me in that moment and led me to also ask if the management company of the building would be willing to renovate a three-bedroom apartment to be wheelchair accessible if such an apartment did not already exist in the building.

Within hours of sending my first batch of e-mails, I received a few responses saying that yes, they would be willing to renovate an existing apartment and asking me to schedule a tour of the building to discuss my access needs. I was astonished and excited by the responses I received. Even after scheduling the tours, however, I was a bit dubious about whether these meetings would actually happen. I remembered the disappointment I felt a year earlier, when leasing agents at several buildings canceled just hours before the tour was meant to start.

But this time around, every tour I scheduled happened. I arranged all of my tours to take place on one of four days. On the first day of tours, I was scheduled to visit two apartment buildings, but I woke up to torrential rain and unseasonably cold temperatures. The weather was supposed to remain the same throughout the day.

The weather conditions gave me pause because of the type of CP I have. If I become cold or wet, one of two things happen: either the spasticity in my muscles increases like nobody's business, which makes moving incredibly difficult and energy consuming, or my muscles cramp, making movement impossible and causing intense pain. If I become cold and wet, that's an entirely different ballgame. To be cold and wet as a person living with CP is to say to each and every muscle in their body, "Muscles, feel free to completely ignore everything I want you to do for the next 24 hours and yes, hurt like you have never hurt before." Although I knew the consequences, I kept my appointments to tour both buildings.

The monsoon-like weather and frigid temperatures were trying to tell me these two buildings were not for me. I discovered this when my caregiver, Kathy, and I arrived at the first building to find that there was no wheelchair-accessible parking. Kathy had to help me get out of her car and into my wheelchair in the middle of the street. When I asked the leasing agent about the location of wheelchair-accessible parking for residents of the building, I was told that the accessible spaces were three or four blocks away, but that's okay because people "like me" don't go out anyway. Strike one . . . I knew this was not my next home.

When Kathy and I arrived at the next building, the leasing agent met us outside and said we had to use the "garbage door." Since it was raining pretty hard, I was certain I didn't hear her correctly and asked her to repeat herself. She said that we had to use the garbage door to enter the building because the only ramp I could use to enter the building was the garbage dumpster ramp, which was located on a secluded side street without streetlights. Say what you like, but I don't do garbage doors nor garbage dumpster ramps. If I'm going to live in a building, I expect to enter and exit the building safely and with other people, not trash. Strike two.

I was officially oh-for-two after my first day of apartment hunting. But I wasn't concerned. I still had three more days of tours ahead. Surely, I'd find something perfect for me.

After two more days of tours, my certainty began to diminish. The apartments I visited were either in not-so-great neighborhoods, suddenly more expensive after I arrived than they were when I arranged the tour, or so inaccessible that the entire apartment would have to be gutted and completely redesigned for me. I had one tour scheduled for my last day of apartment visits. The night before my last tour, I was hopeful but apprehensive.

On my fourth and final day of apartment tours, I woke up with a feeling I can only describe as "awesomeness." The weather was sunny, warm, and dry, so my muscles were in seventh heaven! As Kathy and I got on the road, we noticed that the drive to this apartment building was the smoothest drive we had over the four days of tours. There was no traffic, no road construction necessitating a detour, and we stayed on one main street for the bulk of the drive.

Once we were in the vicinity of the building, I began looking for a parking space on nearby streets, remembering how finding parking at the other apartment buildings had been a struggle. When we were within feet of the building and I still hadn't found a parking spot, I became concerned. However, once we drove closer to the building, I saw a parking lot with wheelchair-accessible parking directly in front of the building. I was absolutely floored.

I pointed to the parking lot and said, "We can park right there!"

Kathy quickly turned in to the lot and said, "That's the easiest parking we've had!"

The leasing agent met us at the main entrance to the building and took us to the apartment that I was interested in. He opened the door and all I saw was a wall. The wall was so close to the door that Kathy barely had enough room to get my wheelchair through the doorway.

After a few minutes of trying to angle my chair just right to get me into the apartment without scuffing the wall, we finally made it into the entryway of the apartment. From here, I could see the soaring ceilings and spaciousness of the living room. I gasped and let out my trademark Allison squeal of excitement. Kathy pushed me into the living room, where I saw a wall of windows that let in tons of natural light and overlooked a bike path and a small park.

Since I was thoroughly impressed by the living room, we went to look at the master bedroom. The bedroom was the perfect size and had one huge window that looked onto the same bike path and some trees.

Although I was in love with the views from, and the spaciousness of, the apartment, I knew that the test of whether I'd be able to live in this apartment comfortably would be the size of the bathroom. Since I need assistance in the bathroom, having a bathroom large enough to fit both my caregiver and me is critical. Most of the bathrooms we saw in previous apartment buildings were just big enough for my wheelchair, but did not have enough room for my caregiver to be in the bathroom with me.

As the leasing agent opened the bathroom door, I held my breath and did my version of crossing my fingers, which amounts to me tightening my fists and squinting my eyes. Kathy carefully pushed me into the bathroom, where we discovered that we both fit and Kathy had plenty of room to move around me.

I was so excited that I turned to the leasing agent and said, "I definitely want this apartment! I absolutely love it!"

After looking at the rest of the apartment, the leasing agent escorted us to his office where we discussed the details of how to turn a beautiful, yet completely inaccessible, space into a home where I could be safe and free to live my life. To my surprise, he had a Reasonable Accommodations

Form, which is a form that a disabled person fills out to request disability-related modifications for her apartment, on his desk with a pen next to it. Although I have filled out a few of these forms over the years, this would be my first time filling out the form for a completely inaccessible apartment. To ensure that I requested everything necessary, I had to do a detailed assessment of every inch of the place. Knowing that this assessment would take time, I asked if I could fill out the form at home and e-mail it back to him. The leasing agent agreed, and Kathy and I left the building.

Once in the car, I couldn't contain my excitement any longer, and I did what anyone would do in this situation: I had a dance party! Kathy turned on the radio and started dancing with me.

"Oh my goodness! I think we did it! I think we have *finally* found my new home," I said between peals of giggles and dancing.

That evening, I worked on the Reasonable Accommodations Form. During the tour, I mentally noted all the inaccessible features of the apartment. Once at home, I divided the features into two lists: features that were inconvenient but safe and features that were unsafe. I only requested modifications for the unsafe features on the form. The next afternoon, I e-mailed the form to the leasing agent. Even though I knew that some of the modifications I requested would require substantial renovation of the apartment, which often meant that the request would be denied, deep in my spirit I just felt that everything would work out perfectly.

A few days after submitting the form, I opened my e-mail app to see that I had received a message from the leasing agent. To say I was nervous would have been like saying the Grand Canyon is a microscopic dent in the Earth. Before opening it, I reminded myself that God organizes everything to work together for my ultimate joy. So, I need not be nervous because whatever was in the e-mail was in my best interest. After my pep talk with myself, I opened the e-mail to find that all of my requested accommodations had been approved! It was official! After years of waiting, wanting, and not knowing how to create a better home for myself, I was going to move to a beautiful home that would be customized for me.

I e-mailed the leasing agent back to express my gratitude and make plans for my move. As soon as I sent the e-mail, I thanked God for this abundance of blessings, grace, and love. As I prayed, I became increasingly excited. By the time I finished the prayer, I was so overjoyed that I had to sit still for fear that I might burst!

Before I knew it, moving day had come! My caregiver, Leslie, had stayed with me overnight and was going to be my right-hand person for the entire day. My mom and aunt had flown out to help too and arrived at my apartment with the movers. In a matter of hours, the apartment that had been filled with years' worth of my life became completely empty. I could no longer call this space "my apartment." While I had waited for this day for years, now that it was here, I felt like I was on the precipice of an entirely new existence.

As I left my old apartment for the last time, taking the elevator down and saying good-bye to the staff, I felt like I was levitating even though I was strapped into my wheelchair.

When I was in the car, I turned to Leslie and said, "I've gotta do it!"

Leslie, knowing exactly what I meant, smiled, and said, "Go for it!"

I let out a huge scream of delight and said, "Oh my gosh! Oh my gosh! Oh my gosh! Do you know what we're about to do?"

I then proceeded to giggle and scream for a solid two minutes, as was fitting for the momentous occasion. Leslie, who was quite accustomed to my expressions of delight, let me have my moment of absolute bliss. Once I concluded my screams of joy, we drove to my new home.

Upon our arrival, we made our way to the main entrance where we were met by Bill, the manager of the building's maintenance department.

"We've been expecting you," he said, escorting us to my new apartment.

"I'm so excited to finally be here. I know I kept you busy the past few days!" I said so excitedly that I could barely get the words out.

He laughed and said, "Yes, we've been quite busy. But we want to make sure that everything is as you need it. If anything needs adjustment, let us know."

With that, he opened the door to my new home and began explaining all the customized equipment and architecture to me. The very first change I noticed was the obnoxious wall, which had made pushing me into the apartment one of the most difficult feats known to humankind, had been moved. Now, pushing me into my apartment was a breeze.

While the construction team had made every renovation that I requested, I soon learned they made other changes to the apartment too. Changes that I had not asked for, but made the apartment even more accessible. Gone was a low-sitting toilet, and in its place was a higher toilet that would be easier for me to use. The steep incline into the kitchen had been flattened, so now rolling into my kitchen was super easy. I was astonished at how meticulous and forward-thinking the team was in remodeling my apartment.

Every time I noticed something that had been modified that I had not included on the Reasonable Accommodations Form, I would say, "You changed that too?"

Bill would nod his head and say, "Yes. We saw that you hadn't put it on the Accommodations Form, but we figured this change would make things easier for you."

I was speechless. Absolutely speechless. I just kept thanking him for all of the hard work that went into renovating my home. I could barely believe everything that they had done to make this home perfect for me.

After Bill finished teaching me the ins and outs of my home, I went to the leasing office to meet the assistant leasing agent and to fill out paperwork. While gathering the paperwork, she asked, "Are you happy with everything?"

I opened my mouth to say yes; but before I could make a sound, tears began streaming down my cheeks.

"Oh, please excuse the tears," I said. "I'm beyond happy with everything! You all have done more than I ever could have imagined! Thank you!"

"As long as those are happy tears, we welcome them," she said handing me a tissue and smiling.

I was so embarrassed. Here I was, sitting in this woman's office, crying. But I couldn't help it. I was simply overcome by the blessings of God! I never expected to live in an apartment owned by a company that would go to such lengths modifying a space for me. This is just one example of the goodness, grace, and blessings that we align ourselves with when we continually express and feel authentic gratitude.

After completing the paperwork, Leslie and I went back to my new home. After a full day of moving, it was time for me to get ready for bed. As Leslie gathered everything for me to shower and get cozy, I quietly looked out my bedroom window. When I first toured the apartment in the middle of summer, the trees outside were full of beautiful dark-green leaves. By my move-in date in October, many of the trees had shed their leaves, meaning that now I could get a glimpse of what was on the other side.

I immediately noticed something glittering in the midst of the bare branches. I focused my eyes on the sparkles and saw that they seemed to be dancing and moving in unison. "This is interesting," I thought to myself. Then all of the sudden, I realized what I was looking at.

"Mom!" I said, a bit louder than normal.

"Yes, honey," she said as she, my aunt, and Leslie descended upon me, a bit concerned by the urgency of my voice.

I kept my gaze fixed on the shimmering sight among the trees, pointed to the window, and asked, "Is that a river outside my window?"

Everyone turned their heads and looked closely at the scene.

My mom smiled and said, "Yes, it is. You can see the river from your bedroom window."

At this point, I was in awe and utter disbelief! I wondered, "How did this happen? How did I go from looking at a huge, gray cement parking garage from my bedroom window to looking at a river from the comfort of a home that was designed for me?"

It was almost more than I could fathom. But I remembered that in the year leading up to my move, I had spent more and more time expressing deep gratitude—even gratitude for that same highly undesirable view at a different angle—and as Iyanla Vanzant, writes, "Gratitude is like a magnet; the more grateful you are, the more you will receive to be grateful for."[2] As you spend more time expressing gratitude, you spend more time feeling abundance, joy, harmony, and so many other feelings that are the very essence of God. When you feel these feelings, you are not only sending a signal to your subconscious that you have received these feelings, but you are also communing with God. The more time you spend in communion with God, the more expansive your subconscious becomes because you are soaking it in the infinite possibilities and infinite intelligence of God. As your subconscious soaks in the realm of infinite possibilities, it and God co-create situations for you to receive more.

The subconscious is like a sponge, and the realm of the Divine is like an infinite pool of love, blessings, intuition, abundance, and so much more. When you express gratitude, you are entering the realm of the Divine. The more time you spend expressing gratitude, the more deeply you submerge your subconscious into the realm of the Divine. The longer it remains in that realm, the more your subconscious absorbs the qualities, and the very essence, of the Divine. As your subconscious becomes completely saturated, and overflowing, with the essence of God, out pours the love, intelligence, and creative power of the Divine onto every area of your life; thus, you will receive more goodness, including insights that are more creative and more expansive than ever before.

This quality of creative expansion is what allowed me to suddenly realize that I could ask if an inaccessible apartment could be renovated for me. Prior to engaging in a practice that required prolonged feelings of gratitude,

I had a subconscious that held the belief that only apartments that were already accessible were possibilities for me. This belief resulted from my experience of never living in an apartment that became accessible at my request. However, by engaging in prolonged periods of gratitude, my subconscious absorbed more of God's qualities, such as infinite possibilities, which expanded my subconscious beyond my previous experiences and ushered me into greater alignment with the infinite blessings of the Divine.

Before concluding this chapter, I want to address the enormous elephant in the room. Although engaging in a gratitude practice is overflowing with gifts from the Divine, expressing gratitude for assistance can be a touchy subject for some with disabilities for a host of reasons. Some people with disabilities feel that they are expected to say thank you for things that those without disabilities aren't expected to say thank you for. Others with disabilities feel that if they say thank you for everything that they receive help with, they may not have energy or time to say anything else. And yet another section of the disability community have been required to express gratitude to simply have their basic needs met. With such a loaded relationship with gratitude, I understand some people's aversion to the whole gratitude thing. So, I offer the following perspectives.

First, regardless of disability status, if you are an adult, no one has the right to your gratitude. Period. However, if you are in a situation where someone is demanding your gratitude and your safety is at risk, choose to see yourself as extending God's grace to the person and say thank you with as much sincerity as possible so that you can get yourself to a safe place. Once you are secure, reach out for help.

Second, simply living with a disability can be a spiritual practice if you choose to see it as such. If you have a disability that necessitates receiving assistance, you have the opportunity to engage in a fertile, rich, and active gratitude practice just by living your life well. You don't have to seek out a practice or figure out a way to incorporate a new practice into your already busy schedule. You can seize the multiple opportunities afforded to you by your disability to express deep gratitude to others throughout your day. By virtue of your disability and the perspective you choose to adopt, you can expand your awareness of your connection to the Divine during your day-to-day activities.

Here's one way to incorporate this concept into your daily routine. If you need assistance to shower, instead of saying thank you for each task that your caregiver does to help you shower, once you have completed your shower, you can say to your caregiver, "Thank you for such a wonderful shower. Your skill at helping me shower has me feeling like a million bucks, and I really appreciate everything you do to help me feel this way!" Of course, you can tweak the wording to work for you.

Now that we've given that elephant some attention, I end this chapter with the following spiritual truth: since God is infinite and creates infinitely, anything you desire, that is in alignment with your highest good, is already waiting for you. You only need to feel and express sustained gratitude for the blessings that already surround you and be receptive to the infinite flow of abundance that God is always pouring upon you, like a shimmering river passing your bedroom window.

HOW TO BE GRATEFUL

Exercises and Prompts

While there are many gratitude exercises, you want to find the exercise that helps you feel gratitude deeply for a prolonged period of time, such as five minutes or more. Finding the right exercise for you may take a few tries, but keep at it. The first exercise I tried was keeping a gratitude journal, which required me to type 10 things I was grateful for every day. Due to the type of cerebral palsy I have, typing is painful and tiring. So, although keeping a gratitude journal helps many people feel and express deep levels of gratitude, the exercise made me feel pain and fatigue—not quite the emotions I was hoping for. I tried different gratitude practices until I found the one that worked for me. I encourage you to try each exercise listed below and determine which one is most effective for you.

Exercise 1: Find what you are grateful for.

If you authentically want to begin a gratitude practice, but just can't think of anything to be grateful for, the following exercise created by Jim Kwik, author of *Limitless,* may help. It gets your gratitude juices flowing by helping you see all the blessings you have in your life at this very moment.

a. Begin by setting a timer for five minutes.
b. Then, pretend that anything you do not say thank you for in the next five minutes will disappear overnight and you will wake up tomorrow morning without it. For example, if you don't say thank you for your body, you will

wake up without a body. If you don't say thank you for the oxygen in the air, you will wake up without oxygen, and so on.

Exercise 2: Keep a daily gratitude journal.

There are various types of gratitude journals, so I'll highlight a few here:

a. The traditional way to keep a gratitude journal is to write down 10 things that you are grateful for every day. Try to avoid writing the same 10 things every day. Some suggest that you write all 10 things at night before you go to bed; while others suggest writing down five things in the morning when you wake up and five things at night before you go to bed. But the most important part of any spiritual practice is consistency, so find the schedule that enables you to consistently write in your journal.
b. The second way to keep a gratitude journal is rooted in the visual arts. If you enjoy drawing or painting, then spend 10 minutes, or more, creating a visual representation of what you are grateful for that day. You need not draw or paint 10 different images (although you can if you like), but you should feel deep gratitude while you are creating your work.
c. The third way to keep a gratitude journal is through photography. If you enjoy taking pictures, then take between three and five digital pictures (on your smartphone or tablet) of things you are grateful for, or items that

represent what you are grateful for, throughout the day. At the end of each day, open a blank document and spend a few minutes creating a montage of your gratitude pictures for the day. As you place each picture in its place in your montage, say out loud or in your mind why the picture makes you feel gratitude.

Exercise 3: Do the Rampage of Appreciation as taught by Esther and Jerry Hicks.

a. Before you begin, think of four or five things that you are grateful for and want to include in your Rampage. It's okay to include other things in your Rampage once you get going.
b. Set a timer for 10 minutes.
c. Say what you are grateful for and why you are grateful for it for 10 minutes. You can say things such as, "I'm grateful for the beautiful sky because I enjoy looking at the glorious colors. I'm grateful for my favorite hobby because it brings me so much joy. I'm grateful for my child's adorable giggle because hearing it always makes me laugh." The most important part of this practice is that you feel completely immersed in gratitude for the entire 10 minutes.

Exercise 4: Express deep gratitude to others throughout your day.

Instead of just saying a quick "Thanks" to someone and continuing with your day, Emiliana Simon-Thomas, Ph.D., a cognitive psychologist, suggests saying thank you using the following three steps.[3]

a. First, describe what the person did that was helpful to you.
b. Second, acknowledge the effort that the person put into doing the task for you.
c. Third, describe how you benefited from the person's behavior.

ACCESS NOTES

Exercise 2: Keep a daily gratitude journal.

1. *If you want to write/type in a traditional gratitude journal but have difficulty typing and/or writing,* try the following modifications and determine which one enables you to feel the most grateful.

   a. Type or write one word that represents each of the 10 items that you are including in your journal. After you type each word, think about why you are grateful for it.

   b. Each time you write in your journal, you can include four or five items, instead of 10.

   c. Write in your journal weekly or biweekly.

2. *If writing/typing in a journal is not possible and you communicate via sign language or speaking,* try the following. Make either a sign language journal where you record videos of yourself signing what you are grateful for or make a voice journal where you say what you are grateful for into a device that records your voice. You can determine how often to make recordings.
3. *If you communicate using symbols on communication cards instead of spoken or typed words,* try the following exercise.

   a. Get a decorative plastic bowl or keepsake box.

   b. Either draw, or print out from a computer, images that symbolize gratitude to you.

   c. Attach these images to the outside of your bowl/box—you have created a gratitude container!

   d. Get a deck of communication cards that you will use only for your gratitude practice.

   e. When you want to express gratitude, choose the card(s) from your communication deck that reflect what you are grateful for and put the card(s) into your gratitude container.

   f. You can choose how many cards you put in your gratitude container and how long you leave the cards in the container.

   g. If you are able, after putting your cards in your gratitude container, either put your hands on one of the gratitude pictures affixed to the outside of your container for a few seconds, or say thank you in your head.

Exercise 3: Do the Rampage of Appreciation as taught by Esther and Jerry Hicks.

4. *If you want to do the Rampage of Appreciation and are unable to speak for 10 consecutive minutes,* here are two alternative ways of doing the exercise.

    a. First, instead of verbally saying everything you are thankful for and why, say what you are grateful for and why in your mind for 10 minutes. When doing the Rampage in this manner, be sure to deeply feel gratitude.

    b. Second, verbally say what you are grateful for and why for less than 10 minutes. Determine the length of time that works best for you and your abilities.

Exercise 4: Express deep gratitude to others throughout your day.

5. *If you want to express deep gratitude to others throughout your day, and you need a shortened version of what to say,* read on. You can say, "Thank you for helping me with *fill in the blank*. Your help makes me feel *fill in the blank*." As you communicate this message, feel deep gratitude.

CHAPTER SEVEN

service

In the mortal world, what I give away is no longer mine.
In the spiritual world, only what I give away is mine.
If I give love, then I shall know love.[1]

— MARIANNE WILLIAMSON

When I was 11 years old, I attended a church service in which the minister told the following story:

> *A man was tending a community garden located in the middle of a bustling city. The garden was beautiful. It was filled with gorgeous, fragrant flowers of various kinds and beautiful fruits and vegetables. Another man was out for a walk and stopped when he saw the lush garden. The man going for a walk yelled to the man tending the garden, "You and God have done wonders with this garden." The man tending the garden said, "You should have seen this place when God was taking care of it alone."*

The minister went on to teach us that God has a Divine plan, and He needs our help to fulfill that plan. I have heard many sermons in my life, but that one has stayed in the forefront of my mind for the rest of my life because it changed my view of my relationship with the Divine.

I have known from the time I was a teeny, tiny child that I was meant to have cerebral palsy (CP) so that I could do my part to improve the world by advocating for, and showing the abilities of, those living with disabilities. The community garden story not only crystallized that belief, but expanded it because it taught me that I, Allison Victoria Thompkins, was chosen to help God carry out Its plan in my own way. On that day, I realized that God needs me, *me*, to help fulfill Its plan in a way that only I can. And this isn't unique to me. Each of us has a form of service that we can engage in to help bring God's plan to fruition.

God's plan for the Universe is one of love, joy, peace, beauty, blessings, abundance, people knowing the truth of who they are, and so many other qualities. However, humans must help God realize Its plan by being of authentic service—that is, serving for the mere joy of serving—to something greater than themselves. Now you might be thinking, "But Allison, there's plenty of places in the world where I don't see evidence of God's plan being fulfilled. What say you about that?" If God's plan is not being fulfilled, God can rectify it, but as Marianne Williamson writes, "We cannot save the world without God's help, but He can't save the world without ours. We need His love; He needs our hands and feet."[2]

When we give our hands and feet in authentic service to a cause, we are caring for that cause, which means that we are allowing the energy of love to flow through us to another entity. Since God is pure love, we are allowing God to flow through us. By allowing God to flow through us, we are circulating the power and the presence of God.

We are, in fact, allowing ourselves to be instruments of the Divine. And when you allow yourself to be an instrument of the Divine, you are embodying your oneness with the Divine. From that place of unity, you can co-create with God grace-filled experiences for those you are serving . . . and for yourself.

I absolutely loved going to camp as a little one, and by the age of 12, I fancied myself a camp connoisseur. One of my favorites was a sleepaway camp in Maine called Agassiz Village. All the campers with disabilities were housed together, and there were three other groups of nondisabled campers ages 7 to 15. Most of the nondisabled campers were of color and came from challenging backgrounds of poverty or being in the foster care system or being labeled "at risk" for a host of other reasons. As a child, I was blissfully unaware of the challenges faced by the vast majority of the nondisabled campers.

During my second summer attending this camp, I got to see the staff talent show—nicknamed "Staff Follies"—for the first time and had a blast. I saw counselors known to be disciplinarians do comedy routines. The camp chefs put on awesome dance routines to the campers' favorite songs. Other camp staff performed hilarious skits, and one of my favorite counselors sang a song that brought down the house with 200 kids cheering him on like he was a rockstar.

While Staff Follies elicited laughter, excitement, and pure, rambunctious, joyous energy from the campers, the performance I remember most was given by a teenage counselor who worked with the youngest nondisabled campers. When the time came for her to perform, she quietly stood up, walked to the make-shift stage in the middle of the dining hall, and just stood there for a few moments. She had on a beautiful long dress and her head was wrapped in a scarf with African print. While we waited for her to begin her performance, the room was completely silent and still.

After a few moments, she lifted the mic to her mouth and began reciting a poem by Nikki Giovanni. I don't remember the name of the poem, but I do remember the poise, the pride, and the presence that counselor exuded during the performance. It was beautiful, awesome, and something completely different from the loud, boisterous energy that the other performers had cultivated. I loved the dancing and singing that came before, but as I listened to her clear voice, I felt the power of the written word in a way I never had in my 12 years of life.

Her performance showed me that strength and beauty reside within all of us, and they need not be demonstratively shown to be undeniably felt. I didn't say a word, but that night I promised myself that I'd show others what she had shown me. If I ever had the opportunity to be a camp counselor, I would somehow show my campers the beauty, grace, power, and fierce intelligence of people of color and of those with disabilities.

Five years later, it was the summer after my junior year of high school, and my turn had finally arrived: I had been hired by Easterseals' camping department to be a counselor at Agassiz Village. As I packed, all of the usual items went into my bag: shorts, shirts, swimsuits, swim shoes, sun visors, *tons* of mosquito repellent, on and on. But I also scanned my bookshelf for just the right book of poetry to add to my growing mound of Maine-bound items. I remembered the promise I made to myself as a 12-year-old. If I had the opportunity, I was going to read a poem at Staff Follies and hopefully, inspire my campers the way I had been inspired. I had a few books to choose from and selected a book of poetry written by a poet of color. Since I had just received this book the previous Christmas, I hadn't actually read it yet. I just packed it and figured that I would find time to read it and select a poem during my days off at camp.

Before I knew it, I was in Maine and fully submerged in the routines of camp life. Singing songs, playing card games, giving out copious hugs, and enjoying absolutely everything about my camp-filled days. Although I was busy with my campers, I was still waiting to hear about the Staff Follies.

I was beginning to doubt that we'd have them at all when finally, about a week and a half before the end of camp, the moment that I had waited five years for arrived: the camp director announced Staff Follies sign ups! The very day it was announced, I found the counselor who was coordinating and proudly stated, "I'd like to sign up to perform!" I was elated and felt like I had planted an invisible flag, staking my claim to the stage.

"Oh, that's great, Allison! I'll add your name to the list. What are you going to do?" he asked.

"I'm reading a poem," I answered.

"What poem?"

"Well, I don't exactly know yet. Is that okay?"

"Oh yeah. That's fine. Just let me know when you know."

And with that exchange, I was off to find the perfect poem for Staff Follies. I spent my time off reading through the book of poetry I had brought from home and realized one thing: I was in huge trouble!

The poems in this book fit into one of two categories: really boring esoteric poetry or really, *really* boring esoteric poetry. I dog-eared the pages with the least-boring poems, but my goal was to inspire the campers, not put them to sleep. I knew that if I read one of these poems at Staff Follies, I'd probably have to read it standing on my head while twirling a Hula-Hoop around one of my ankles to keep the kids' attention. Since my balance on two feet was iffy, I figured that testing my balance by standing on my head wouldn't be the wisest thing. I knew I had to come up with plan B and fast. But how? I was at a camp in the middle of rural Maine and the Internet was not as ubiquitous as it is now. Thus, I had zero idea of how to get access to more poetry by poets of color.

After realizing that I was in a poetry pickle, I decided to go for a roll in my motorized wheelchair and ended up going to the space designated as the hangout cabin for the teen counselors and kitchen staff. We had a television, pool table, and a few couches in there. During our time off, we'd go there to socialize, relax, and just be teenagers.

On this particular day, the cabin was hopping. A few people were playing an intense pool game, the movie *Friday* was being shown for the umpteenth time that summer, and some girls were talking while braiding their hair. I drove my wheelchair into this hotbed of activity and parked next to one of the couches, ready to watch the movie. However, as I parked my chair next to one of the couches, a small, pink-and-green paperback book caught my attention. I picked it up and saw that it was a book entitled *Poems* by Dr. Maya Angelou. I quickly skimmed through the book and thought, "This could be my plan B!"

I held up the book and asked, "Does anyone know whose book this is?"

With permission from the book's owner—a supervisor named Aaron—I was back in the game, but I was now under a serious time crunch. Staff Follies was in six days!

In that time, I had to read through this book, pick a poem, and rehearse the poem. Oh, and I was still a full-time counselor. I was not sure when I'd find the time to do all of this, but I was excited nonetheless.

For the first two days that the book was in my possession, my eyes were glued to it whenever I had a free moment. I immersed myself in its pages. I went to sleep well after my self-imposed bedtime, set my alarm clock to wake me up earlier than normal each morning, and when the campers had rest hour after lunch, I had "read Dr. Angelou's book nonstop" hour.

During the first 48 hours, nothing jumped out at me. While her poems were beautiful and powerful, I simply didn't find one that said, "Allison, stop reading now! I AM the poem you've been looking for!"

On the third day of having this book, I woke up early again and began reading. I was becoming impatient and began to think, "Maybe I've set the bar too high. Maybe I just need to pick a random poem and hope for the best. After all, I read a few poems that I liked. Maybe I should just go with one of those and stop looking for something that really resonates with me." I resolved to read five more poems, and if nothing spoke to me, I'd simply choose one of Dr. Angelou's poems that I liked.

I returned to reading the book, and the first poem still did not speak to me, so I turned the page. The poem on this page was titled "Phenomenal Woman." As I read the poem, I became more and more excited. This one spoke to me! Finally, I found a poem that I could envision myself reciting, that had fun imagery for the campers, that was uplifting, and that spoke to the beauty, power, grace, and awesomeness that everyone has inside of them. *This was it! This was the poem!*

Except for one small, itsy, bitsy problem: the poem contained words such as *breast*, and some of the campers were as young as seven years old. Even though I knew that many of the campers heard, and used, language far more risqué than the words in the poem, I wanted to be careful about the language I used with such a young audience.

I knew for a fact that this was *the poem*, so I decided that I would not recite the lines of the poem that seemed a bit mature. Fortunately, there were only a few lines that fell into this category.

With the poem chosen and three days until my debut in Staff Follies, there was only one thing to do: rehearse like nobody's business! I kept the same schedule that I had adopted when looking for the poem and used it to rehearse the poem. During my rehearsals, I decided which words to stress, what movements to make to emphasize certain ideas and what tone to use to bring levity to certain lines and seriousness to others. It was awesome, and I became increasingly excited to recite the poem as my performance took shape.

The day of Staff Follies arrived, and I was so excited to get up onstage that I felt like a kid myself. Before the show, the coordinator took me aside to ask if I needed anything for my performance and I was so relieved. I had been so busy being a counselor and preparing my performance that I hadn't asked for the disability accommodations I needed to actually participate in Staff Follies. Oops! He took notes as I requested a mic stand and someone to hold the book for me. It was all becoming so real.

As the campers entered the dining hall that evening, a buzz of anticipation permeated the air. The kids were eager to be entertained by their counselors and wondered what they had planned. The counselors were working out last-minute details behind the scenes and scurrying around to ensure that the kids were settled in their seats.

As I watched my fellow staff members perform, I became increasingly nervous and began doubting myself. Watching the campers thoroughly enjoy all of the singing, dancing, and hilarious skits, I thought, "What on Earth am I doing? I'm going to go on that stage, start reading my poem, and the kids are going to be bored to bonkers! They'll probably yell, 'Get that lady off the stage! We want more music!'"

Just as my thoughts began to spiral, I remembered being that 12-year-old camper in awe of the counselor who could command the stage by simply reading a poem. That reminder was the Divine speaking to me through my memory, reassuring me that reading this poem was the right path for me. Although I didn't know how the poem would be received, I could be at peace knowing that all would be okay.

In a blink of an eye, or so it seemed, the person scheduled to perform before me had finished their performance, and I heard the emcee say, "Next, we have Allison from the Explorer section who will read 'Phenomenal Woman' by Maya Angelou."

I drove onto the stage. The emcee adjusted the microphone stand to my height, and Aaron knelt down next to me. He found the poem in the book, held up the book so I could see it, and gave me a wink. I smiled, took a deep breath, and looked around the room to see the entire camp looking at me.

It was a beautiful late August evening. The campers and counselors were seated in a U-shape around the stage. Campers with disabilities were seated in front of me. Behind me was a wall of windows that let in the soft golden light of the setting sun. After taking in the beauty of the moment, I began to perform the poem.

I performed it just like I rehearsed it. I tossed my head back in all the right places. I leaned forward in my wheelchair as if I was telling them a secret just like I wanted. I motioned with my hands and shoulders to emphasize the playful tone of some of the lines. I said the lines, "'Cause I'm a woman / Phenomenally. / Phenomenal woman, / That's me," with all the sass, gumption, and attitude that I had practiced. I looked into the eyes of as many campers as I could. I felt so great up on that stage that I took a bit of poetic license and added the word *yeah* to a few lines of the poem. I was in my element!

I felt like the phenomenal woman I was speaking about. I embodied that woman and did my best to convey to the kids that they were phenomenal young women and young men too. We are all phenomenal. That night I knew that when one person embraces and exudes her phenomenal nature, others feel it and they feel liberated to embrace and exude their own phenomenal nature. I embraced and exuded my phenomenal nature in the hopes that a few of the kids would do the same.

As I read the closing lines, I simply hoped that the campers had enjoyed my performance and that at least one of them gained a newfound, or deeper, understanding of her or his own beauty, intelligence, and power. When I was done, I let out a quiet giggle. I had fulfilled my promise to myself: I gave the campers a moment to reflect.

I received the usual round of applause as I drove off the stage. I gave the book back to Aaron and thanked him for letting me borrow it.

He said, "Allison, that was amazing!"

I thanked him again and drove back to my seat with my campers. But before I got there, one of the teen counselors, who was known for his stoic and quiet demeanor, stopped me and said, "You did your thing up there!" and gave me a huge bear hug. Apparently, he liked my performance too.

"Well, if I didn't reach any of the campers at least I know that two of the counselors really liked it," I thought to myself.

After my bear hug, I sat with my campers and watched the remaining performances. At the end of the Follies, the lights turned on and one of my campers turned to me and said, "I liked your poem. I really like how you said, 'Yeah, I'm phenomenal!'" This camper also used a wheelchair and said the words, "Yeah, I'm phenomenal," with all of the sass that I had said it with. She even put her hands on her hips and leaned forward in her chair.

As I was helping my campers get ready to leave the dining hall, I realized that it was completely dark outside. I checked my watch and saw that my workday was officially done. My friend Naveed, who was also a teen counselor and used a wheelchair, and I decided to hang out in the dining hall for a while. He had also participated in Staff Follies with a group of counselors who performed a rap song. As we talked about the show, I mentioned that I hoped the campers weren't too bored while I read the poem.

Naveed looked at me, almost incredulously, and said, "Allison, the kids couldn't take their eyes off of you. I watched my campers, and they were fidgeting and not paying very close attention to the other acts, but when you started talking, they all stopped fidgeting and sat completely still for the whole poem."

"They did? I didn't notice that."

"You were kinda busy up there," he said, giving me a wry smile, "but I noticed. Allison, these kids were mesmerized by what you did. They'll remember that poem for the rest of their lives."

Since Naveed and I had met as preteens years earlier and now worked as counselors together, I figured he was being an awesome friend by assuring me that the kids enjoyed my performance. I doubted that the kids enjoyed the poem that much, but I so appreciated Naveed's support that I allowed myself to bask in his words.

The next morning, I awoke to one of my co-counselors' gently nudging me. I was so sound asleep that I had slept through my alarm. After my co-counselor helped me get ready for the day, I headed out the door of my cabin to go to the activity that I was assigned to: Rhythm and Drama. Since I tire more easily than those without cerebral palsy, one of the workplace accommodations that I negotiated with my lead counselor was being allowed to sleep in. So, instead of getting up before the campers and helping them get dressed and eat breakfast, I woke up after the campers and met them after breakfast.

This meant that when I left my cabin each morning, campers were milling around camp going to their various activities. The morning after Staff Follies was no different. When I left my cabin, I saw groups of campers going here, there, and everywhere. I smiled and waved at them, as I did every morning. However, something strange happened when I waved to the first group.

"It's her! It's the phenomenal woman! Hi, phenomenal woman!" said two little girls as they ran over to me.

For a moment, I had absolutely no idea who they were talking to, so I looked around, and then I suddenly realized that they were greeting me. They remembered the poem from the night before!

I smiled and said, "Hi." I proceeded to give them both a hug and sent them on their way.

As I continued driving my wheelchair to the Rhythm and Drama cabin, I chuckled to myself, only to hear a chorus of older campers say, "Hi, phenomenal woman."

"Hi, girls!" I said as my smile grew.

Right after greeting the older campers, I saw a few campers from the cabin for the youngest children. They looked at me, started grinning and said, "Hi, phe . . . phen . . . phenomedible woman!"

Their counselor, who was with them, slowly said, "Phennommmeennnaall woman."

The kids studied his lips, looked back at me, and tried again: "Hi, phenom . . . phenomen . . . phenomenal woman!"

They started giggling and gave me a hug. "Hi, you two! You did a great job saying that big word!" They smiled and went on their merry way.

For the remaining days of camp, I was officially the "Phenomenal Woman." I almost called my parents to tell them that my name was no longer Allison because my campers had renamed me "Phenomenal Woman." I know for a fact that some of those children had never even heard the word *phenomenal* before Staff Follies, and now they were saying it with joy and exuberance in everyday conversation.

When you engage in authentic service, you allow your intuition, which is God's voice within you, to tell you how you can best serve others. As Dr. Paul Masters writes,

> *When God's presence within you intuitively tells you what will give your life meaning, fulfillment, and thus lasting happiness, it can be taken as fact and lived out to your benefit and that of those around you. You*

will know if it is intuition from God because it will involve the good of others as well as yourself.[3]

Throughout my journey of performing "Phenomenal Woman," I listened to my intuition. When I was a 12-year-old camper inspired by my counselor's recitation of a Nikki Giovanni poem, I allowed that inspiration to guide me to recite a poem for my campers. When I read through a book of poetry that was less than exciting, I listened to my intuition and focused on finding another source of poetry. When I found another book of poems, I kept reading poem after poem until I found the right one to perform.

Since I allowed my intuition to be my guiding force in serving my campers, the impact of my poetry reading was far greater than I thought it would be. As it turned out, I was the perfect person to bring that poem to that audience. Part of God's plan is that each of us know the truth of who we are: we are love, intelligence, beauty, joy, and so many other wonderful qualities. By performing "Phenomenal Woman" in a way that resonated with the campers and counselors, I played a role in bringing God's plan to fruition. Since I was the only counselor to read a poem that evening and the only counselor who was a Black disabled woman, I was uniquely, indeed perfectly, positioned to deliver God's message that we are all phenomenal to the campers and counselors at this particular camp. Since most of the campers and counselors shared at least one identity with me, they could see part of themselves in me during my performance and truly believe that they were phenomenal too.

For days after the performance, campers recited the poem back to me. I had simply hoped to give them the moment of reflection and inspiration I had; however, the moment I hoped to give them lasted much longer than I had intended, and the inspiration sunk deeper into their consciousness than I thought it would. In their happy insistence to say "phenomenal woman" every time they saw me, the campers were seeing and reinforcing their own phenomenal nature. How does focusing on someone else's phenomenal nature reinforce your own? When you focus your attention on a quality, be it kindness or love or joy, in someone else, you are expanding that quality within yourself. The kids resonated with my performance so deeply that they were able to see the phenomenal in their everyday lives.

And I benefited too. Before I found that poem, I never associated myself with being phenomenal. I knew I was smart and capable, but at age 17, I was still figuring out who I was and what it meant to be a young African American woman with a significant disability. Sure, I could do a lot, but I was one year away from going off to college to begin my independent life, and I was filled with questions about how I would succeed. As I performed the poem, I did my best to fully embody the words of the poem so that the campers would enjoy themselves and see their own phenomenal nature. However, I did not expect the kids to see my phenomenal nature. I did not expect to be reminded from that night forward that not only did I read "Phenomenal Woman," but that I was one. That although I may have challenges to overcome and I may need assistance to live the life that I envisioned for myself, I could live that life because I am a phenomenal woman! To be reminded of that fact by the very people who I sought to inspire is a gift that I cherish to this day.

But you see, that is what can happen when you engage in the spiritual practice of authentic service to others. Yes, you improve the lives of others by the action you take and by the love you circulate while engaging in the activity. However, since we are all connected, as you pour love into others through your service, love is poured right back into you, which magnifies the Divine within you. As the Divine within you is magnified, you become more and more aware of your union with God. From that place of unity, blessings, grace, and the beauty of God Itself radiates through you and your life is simply phenomenal!

HOW TO BE OF SERVICE

Exercises and Prompts

There are as many ways to be of service as there are people on the planet. The key is to find *your* way to serve—that is, the type of service that is fun for you, that feeds your soul, and that simply feels like home to you. If you know what that is for you, fantastic! Go forth and serve! But, if you haven't the faintest idea of how you should serve, keep on reading.

Exercise 1: Pray to be shown the best way for you to serve.

That's right, ask God, the source of all intelligence, to show you how you can best be of service. If you're unsure of what should be included in such a prayer, try the following prayer:

> *Dear God [or whatever word you use to name God], Thank you so much for [name between 3 and 5 things you are grateful for. They can be things such as your favorite shirt in your favorite color or the last time you and your best friend laughed so hard you both turned*

red, or the way the breeze felt on your cheeks the last time you went to the beach. Be as specific as possible and really feel the feelings of joy and gratitude as you list the items]. I know that God is the knower of all things and the source of clarity. And I know that God wants only the best for me. Thus I ask clarity regarding the best way for me to authentically serve. I know that there's a way for me to serve that is filled with fun, joy, harmony, peace, and that uses my abilities perfectly. Lord, please show me how to best serve according to my unique talents, interests, and lifestyle. I love you, God, and I thank you for the clarity that you have revealed to me. In your holiest of names I pray. And so it is. Amen.

Once you have finished praying, remain alert and receptive to any messages that come your way. You may overhear a conversation in which people are discussing the needs of an organization or an individual. You may be asked to help with a project by someone you know or see an opportunity for service on your social media feed, or have a dream, or have a thought about a cool service project. God answers prayers in a myriad of ways, so be open to receiving an answer from anywhere at any time.

Exercise 2: Acquaint yourself with various options for service.

Below are a few options that might be of interest if you are looking for ways to serve your community and the world:

a. *If you graduated from college, contact your Alumni Office* and see if it has opportunities for alums to give back to their college or university.

b. *Alternatively, if you are a college graduate and you come from a minority group* (racial, disability, first-generation college graduate, immigrant, LGBTQ+, etc.), contact the on-campus office responsible for supporting current students with that background and offer to mentor a student or give a speech via Zoom. If you are interested in this option, I recommend being clear on the time you can commit and what you want to do before contacting the office (for example, do you want to mentor a student via telephone, e-mail, Zoom, or in-person? Do you want to be in touch once or more?).

c. *Support an organization that you believe is doing wonderful work.* This can be an organization that you participated in or an organization that you just learned about. You can support the organization by participating in its hashtag campaigns or by telling people about the organization on your social media platforms and including information regarding how your followers can support the organization with their time or money. You can also raise money for the organization through a website, such as GoFundMe.com.

d. *Choose one person* (this person can be someone you know or someone you don't know) and spend 3 to 5 minutes praying for that person's happiness for 7 consecutive days. When you pray for this person, refrain from praying that they receive certain things, such as a car or a house or a job. Instead, pray that the person experiences more qualities such as love, joy, harmony, blessings, abundance, and health than ever before. When you pray for someone to experience qualities, you leave the door open for circumstances to transpire in whatever way necessary for that person to experience those qualities. Read the chapter titled Prayer to learn more about this principle. If you need an idea of what to say in your prayer, see below:

Dear God [or whatever word you use to name God], Thank you so much for [say between 3 and 5 things you are grateful for about that person. They can be things such as the person's personality traits that you admire, or specific achievements that person has accomplished, or the way you feel when you're in that person's presence. As you say whatever you are thankful for about the person, be as specific as possible and really feel the feelings of joy and gratitude as you list the items]. I know that you God are pure love, the source of all blessings, and the knower of my deepest desires. And I know that you want only the best for me and for [say the name of the person you are praying for]. It is from this place of love and blessings that I pray [say the name of the person who you are praying for] experiences and is one with all of the happiness, joy, peace, blessings, and abundance that are naturally hers/his/theirs as a child of the Most High. I pray Lord that You soak him/her/them through and through with your grace, with your love, and with your Divine blessings. I pray, Lord, this person is enveloped in your presence in a way she/they/he has never been before and as a result feels more joy, more beauty, more harmony, more abundance, more grace, and more synchronicities than he/she/they ever knew was possible. I pray these blessings and even more goodness pour down upon her/them/him every second of every day for the rest of their/his/her life and forevermore! Thank you so much for answering my prayer beautifully, lovingly, and with all of the grace and joy known in the Divine realm. I love you, God. And so it is. Amen.

Exercise 3: Send handwritten or typed cards to people in your life.

In these cards, tell the person how much they mean to you and why, and end the card with a blessing such as "May you have a beautiful day," or "May you be surrounded by love and harmony," or "May you experience eternal prosperity." You can choose to send one card daily, weekly, or biweekly. You decide what you can handle.

ACCESS NOTES

The above ideas of how to engage in service are meant to be inclusive of those who are unable to leave their homes or their beds.

Exercise 1: Pray to be shown the best way for you to serve.

1. *If you are nonverbal, nonspeaking, or minimally verbal and want to pray,* I suggest doing the following experiment to determine how to make your prayer practice as effective as possible:

a. First, if you use an AAC device with a voice synthesizer, type either part or all of the above prayer into your AAC device. Then, have your device speak the prayer, and as your device is saying the prayer, feel as much passion and emotion as possible.

b. Second, say the prayer in your head with as much passion and emotion as you can.

c. Once you finish, determine which method enabled you to feel your prayer the most deeply. Speaking your prayer is not required to pray effectively; however, deeply feeling the words of your prayer is required for it to be effective. So, you want to select the method of praying (either saying the prayer in your head or having your device speak your prayer) that allows you to most deeply feel your prayer.

2. *If you have Attention Deficit Hyperactivity Disorder (ADHD), want to pray, and have difficulty focusing while praying,* the following suggestions may make prayer more accessible to you.[4]

a. First, try writing out your prayers in advance and then reading what you wrote out loud.

b. You can keep a prayer journal where you write out your prayers or bullet-point lists of things that you want to pray about.

c. Pray in a quiet place in your home. If possible, designate this as your prayer space and don't do anything else in this space. Also, hang a picture that symbolizes spirituality in this space.

d. Before you begin praying, take a few deep breaths to relax your body.

e. Pray while manipulating a fidget toy. God does not care what you are doing with your hands when you pray as long as you are feeling your prayer as deeply as possible.

f. If sitting still while praying is too difficult, try praying while exercising.

Exercise 3: Send handwritten or typed cards to people in your life.

3. *If mailing handwritten or typed cards is difficult or not possible,* you can send e-mails or texts to people in your life. If possible, I'd recommend sending people an e-mail with the same sentiments as noted in Exercise 3 of this chapter. However, if sending an e-mail is not feasible, please feel free to text your message.

CHAPTER EIGHT

connection

The greatest ability is availability.[1]

— REV. MICHAEL BERNARD BECKWITH

The previous chapters in this book have taught you how to incorporate spiritual practices in your life to experience a greater awareness of your connection with God; however, the exercises and techniques I have suggested require people to have some physical and cognitive ability to actively participate. So, some people may be wondering, "Can someone without the physical and/or cognitive ability to initiate a spiritual practice still engage in spirituality?"

Others may be thinking, "This is great info, but I have someone in my life who, by virtue of the severity or nature of her disability, cannot do any of the practices in this book. In fact, I'm doubtful that the person is even aware of the world around him. Can this person be 'spiritual'?" The answer to both questions is a resounding YES! Reports from those who have been in comas explain that these individuals maintain a rich inner life, open to deep inner experiences, including making a spiritual connection.[2]

Every person has the capacity to be spiritual and engage in spiritual practices. However, some people will need to rely on others to bring those spiritual practices into their lives.

God is everywhere, which means that God is in members of the disability community who are in a coma, who are in a persistent vegetative state (PVS), who have locked-in syndrome, or who are minimally conscious. Since God is in these people as well, they can experience oneness with God. They can embody their divinity. Each person has a unique relationship with the Divine that does not depend on physical ability, intellectual prowess, or even awareness of what is happening around them. Instead, the relationship each of us has with God is a direct reflection of who we are, where we are on our spiritual journey, and the love, compassion, and all-knowing intelligence of the Divine. Each human does what she can to connect with God, and God does the rest. Hence, a person in PVS need not write in a gratitude journal to experience oneness with God, nor does a person in a coma need to be of service to others to be in the flow of the Divine. Those with the most severe disabilities can engage in spiritual practice by being surrounded by the energy of spiritual practice.

Just as those who are minimally conscious or who are in a PVS depend on others for their physical needs, those who have the most profound disabilities will need assistance to engage in spiritual practices. This is where you—their loved one, their friend or their spiritual leader—have a vital role to play. You can be the bridge that connects a person with minimal consciousness and/or minimal physical abilities with opportunities to engage in spiritual practice. I have known this since I saw it in action as a 12-year-old participating in a weekly enrichment program, and I have never forgotten.

When I began the seventh grade, my mother learned about a program that was held on Saturday mornings for children who had physical disabilities, intellectual disabilities, or both. I was eager to attend the program, as it would be a fun social activity on the weekends. Since I was now in junior high, I could not be caught at home on the weekends—I had to be cool and be on the go!

On the first day of the program, I was excited to see that I knew many of the other participants. Most of us had gone to Camp Echo Bridge together and remembered each other from the summer. There was one participant, Lilly, who had gone to camp with the rest of us, but who I didn't know very well.

You see, Lilly had the most severe disabilities of any camper at camp. When Lilly was a toddler, she was attacked by a dog, which caused her to have significant brain damage and led her to live with profound disabilities. She used a wheelchair and couldn't move her arms or legs independently. She was unable to speak, make a sound, or communicate. The people around her had to do their best to determine her needs. Her eye gaze was fixed, which means her eyes never moved. She never turned her head, nor did she change her facial expression. She kept the same expression on her face regardless of what was happening around her. She did not respond to anything around her.

Although Lilly didn't have any means of communication, and the other kids and I never knew what Lilly did and didn't understand, we always did our best to include her in our conversations and activities. All of us knew what it felt like to have people ignore us based on their preconceived notions of our disabilities, and we were determined not to do that to Lilly. She may not have been able to interact with us like we could interact with each other, but we were going to make sure we included her as best we could. So, if she showed up to camp with new sunglasses, we all complimented her on her sunglasses. If it was hot outside, Lilly was the first one to know just how hot we were.

The camp counselors were equally inclusive of Lilly. They would talk to her if campers were not talking to her. Whenever we had arts and crafts, the counselors would move her arms and hands so that she was a part of creating art projects. She was fully included in the action of camp.

Naturally, this inclusion continued during the Saturday morning program. All of the participants and program staff would go on nature hikes together, do art projects, make simple recipes, or simply hang out and talk with each other. And Lilly was included in all of it. Sure, a staff member always had to move her and make decisions for her, but Lilly was just as busy as the rest of the kids.

About four weeks into the program, I awoke one Saturday morning to torrential downpours, lightning, and thunder. Concerned that the program might be canceled due to the weather, I asked my mom to call the program director who assured me that the program was still taking place. While that day's program was still scheduled, it was clear that we would have to be indoors for the entire duration of that week's activities. No going on nature walks. No relaxing outside on the grass.

Fortunately, the staff had come up with several wonderful activities for us to do indoors. All the usual participants, including Lilly, came to the program that week. We had fun playing games and making simple snacks for each other. We were hard at work making friendship bracelets when a hush came over the room. Everyone was concentrating on their bracelets and the only time people spoke was when one of the participants needed help. Lilly and I were sitting next to each other, and we each had a staff member assisting us with our bracelets.

One of the staff members decided that the room was way too quiet and turned on some music. This was the first time that music played at the Saturday program, so the other kids and I got excited. I started bopping my head to the beat. The other kids started dancing in their seats and commenting on the music.

As I bopped my head to the beat, I noticed a slight commotion next to me. I turned my head to see Lilly's hand moving back and forth on her lap. I just stared at her hand for a moment, partly not believing what I was seeing and partly excited for Lilly. In the few months I had known Lilly, I had never seen her move her limbs independently. Apparently, I wasn't the only one who had never seen Lilly move under her own power because I overheard Abby, the staff member working with Lilly, tell one of the other staff members to get the program director, Kelly, immediately.

While we waited for the program director, I looked at Lilly's face. She had the same facial expression as always; her eyes were looking in the usual direction. But her hand just kept moving back and forth. As I tried to understand what was happening, Kelly arrived.

"What's going on?" asked Kelly.

"I just looked down at Lilly's hands and her right hand was moving like this. Is it a seizure?" Abby said, a bit panicked.

Kelly looked at Lilly's hand thoughtfully for a moment and asked, "When did this start?"

"I think when we turned on the music," answered Abby.

Kelly continued watching Lilly, and then a light came to Kelly's eyes, along with a huge smile. Kelly sat down, picked up Lilly's moving hand, and placed it in the palm of her hand. As soon as Lilly's hand was in Kelly's hand, Lilly's hand moved back and forth even faster.

"She's not having a seizure. She's dancing," said Kelly. "Turn off the music."

Sure enough, when the music stopped, so did Lilly's hand. When the music turned back on, Lilly's hand began moving again.

Kelly placed Lilly's hand back on her lap and said, "In American Sign Language, the sign for dancing is this," Kelly held her left hand up with the palm facing up and extended her index finger and her middle finger on her right hand to look like an upside-down *V* and swung them back and forth above her left palm.

Lilly could dance! Someone who has disabilities as profound as Lilly's was able to connect with the vibration and energy of music so deeply that it moved her to jam. Lilly was able to express and celebrate life by moving her body in a way that was uniquely her own. Yes, she needed assistance in the form of someone turning on music. But, once that music was on, Lilly simply allowed the love, light, and divinity that was within her to shine forth as she danced her dance.

The staff played music for the rest of the day and Lilly just kept dancing. When Lilly's parents arrived to pick her up from the program, Kelly asked them about Lilly's response to music.

"Oh yes. Lilly loves dancing to her music at home. So, we keep a small radio near her at all times for her to enjoy," explained her dad.

"If you like, you can bring a few of her favorite music tapes every Saturday, and we'll play them throughout each session so she can be more involved," offered Kelly.

"Okay. We'll do that!"

From that day on, whenever possible, one of the staff members turned on one of Lilly's favorite cassette tapes, and Lilly would joyfully dance her dance.

Now, your family member or friend may not be able to respond to spiritual practice like Lilly responded to music, which is okay because there is a common misconception that once the patient is unresponsive there is nothing more happening inside of their brain. Current research shows, however, that those in coma register what is going on around them, they are simply unable to respond in the manner that is expected.[3] Since this is true for those in a coma, which is the most extreme form of reduced consciousness, this is very likely true for some people who are in PVS or who are minimally conscious, which are less severe forms of reduced consciousness. It should be noted that some experience PVS or minimal consciousness as a complete blackout or whiteout. While those experiencing this form of reduced consciousness are not able to register what is happening around them, they do benefit from the energy of spiritual practice that surrounds them. Thus, regardless of the specific form of reduced consciousness your family member or friend may be experiencing, the person will still benefit from being surrounded by an atmosphere of consciously connecting to the Divine. You may never know just how this atmosphere positively impacts the person; that is between God and that individual. But you can rest assured that by providing the person with the opportunity to experience their connection with the Divine, you are providing that person the opportunity to bask in the love, joy, and light of that which created them and demonstrating that spirituality is, in fact, for *every body*. What a beautiful gift!

HOW TO CONNECT

Exercises and Prompts

Although this chapter focuses on how to help others engage in spiritual practices, there are a few steps you should take before assisting someone with severe disabilities with her spiritual practice:

a. First, and foremost, obtain permission to engage in spiritual practice with the person from the disabled person or the person who oversees the care of the disabled person.
b. Second, before you assist someone else in deepening their connection with God, you want to be as aligned with, and in the flow of, the Divine as possible. You can do this by meditating for between 5 and 30 minutes before you go to see the person you will be assisting. Or, right before you go in to the person's room, you can do one of the surrendering-to-God exercises found in this book or say an affirmative prayer.
c. Third, speak to the person in a loving and positive manner.
d. Finally, once you are in the person's presence, explain what you are about to do, why you are going to do it, and ask the person to give you a sign to tell you if he enjoyed the practice

or not. I understand that the person may not be conscious or able to easily communicate, but fully including the person in the practice by explaining the practice and inviting the person to convey whether or not he enjoyed the experience is important as these actions establish the intention that the practice is for that individual.

e. Since most of the people will be unable to speak, use your intuition and watch for signs to determine how the person is feeling.

Exercise 1: Music brings us together.

I'm pretty sure you can guess the first suggestion based on Lilly's love of music! If the person has a favorite spiritual song, or a few favorite spiritual songs, and you are comfortable singing, feel free to sing to the person. If you are uncomfortable singing, then play the songs for the person to hear. If the person can tolerate it, put the radio or music playing device in the bed with the person or on the person's lap so the vibrations of the music can go through the person's body. If you put the music playing device in the person's bed with them, be sure to remove the device when you are done with the music.

Exercise 2: Spiritual imagery and art inspire us.

Find a picture of a spiritual image—such as the tree of life, or the symbol for the third eye, or the symbol for Ohm—or a picture of nature and hang the picture on the wall above the head of the person's bed. If you cannot hang the picture directly above the person's head, hang it as close to the person's bed as you can. If you cannot hang the picture on the wall, tape the picture to the foot of the person's bed or put the picture on a surface near where the person sleeps.

Exercise 3: Meditate with the person.

Bring your favorite guided meditation track or your favorite meditation music and meditate while you are in the person's presence. You may want to try to hold the person's hand as you meditate with them or simply put your hand near the person. While meditating, you may want to put a picture of a spiritual image under the person's hand or on the person's bed or lap.

ACCESS NOTES

Exercise 3: Meditate with the person.

If you need ideas of how to modify meditation to fit your abilities, please refer to the ACCESS NOTES in the Meditation chapter of this book.

final words

Often when we discuss engaging in spiritual practices, people focus on the importance of improving one's own life with these techniques. While this is an important result, it is not the only, or even the most important reason, to engage in spiritual practices.

When you engage in spiritual practice, you improve the world by making the entire cosmos a more loving, harmonious, and joyous place for everyone and everything. As you create a more loving planet through your spirituality, you play a role in bringing the Divine plan to fruition. "How?" you might ask. Have you ever heard of the butterfly effect? This is a theory that states a minor change in one situation in the world can cause a change in a seemingly unconnected situation somewhere else in the world, like the flap of a butterfly's wings causing a typhoon.

This occurs because we are all connected. The Divine that is present in me, is also present in you, is also present in your neighbor, and on and on, linking us together in a complex, interconnected web of energy. While each religion and every person may have a different name for, and understanding of, God, there is only one energy that lights the sun, that beats the heart of every human, that grows a seed into a mighty tree. This one energy is pervasive, and each of us is connected to this energy by virtue of our existence. So, if I engage in spiritual practices that enable me to be more loving, the increased love I feel ripples out from me and increases the total love present in the Universe. When I increase the love, the peace, the joy, and the compassion in my own life, I increase the love, compassion, joy, and peace in other people's lives around the world. We are one. What is felt by one being is felt by all. As Marianne Williamson writes, "The wind currents at the North Pole are affected when a butterfly flaps its wings in South America, and the entire world is affected by every thought you think."[1]

Not only is this phenomenon explained in spiritual terms, it is also understood in scientific terms. Physicists Albert Einstein, Boris Podolsky, and Nathan Rosen wanted to prove that if you put enough distance between two particles that were once joined, the motion of one particle would not be impacted by the motion of the other particle. However, their experiment proved just the opposite. The three physicists conducted an experiment in which they divided one electron into two electrons. Let's name the two electrons S and B. After dividing the electron into two and separating the electrons by a substantial distance, the scientists changed the motion of S by directly touching it. Pretty routine stuff. However, particle B—the particle that was not touched—also changed its motion to match the motion of S. And what is most fascinating is that B changed its motion at precisely the same moment that the motion of S was changed. There was no delay. In quantum physics this phenomenon is called "quantum entanglement."

Originally, this experiment was conducted in the 1930s and subject to the technological constraints of the time. In the decades following the Einstein-Podolsky-Rosen experiment, the process has been replicated many times with different particles and increasingly sophisticated technology that enabled scientists to place particles further apart from each other. Regardless of the distance between the pair of particles and the type of particle used, the experiments demonstrated the same result: when the motion of one particle of the pair was altered, the motion of the other particle in the pair experienced an identical change in its motion.

You might be thinking, "This is a fascinating detour into the physical sciences, Allison, but what on Earth does it have to do with *my* spiritual practices improving the world?" Great question! Whether you believe in the Big Bang theory or you believe that God created the Universe, if you go back far enough in time, you come to a point when the Universe did not exist, and a millisecond later, a burst of energy birthed the entire Universe. That burst of energy, whether Divine or something else, acted upon a single entity and the world was created. This single entity was divided to create planets, stars, and life forms of all types, including human beings. *A Course in Miracles* says, "[The will of God] encompasses all things because it created all things. By creating all things, it made them part of itself. . . . You are part of [God]." Hence, when a human being changes their "motion" by engaging in a spiritual practice that causes them to be more loving or peaceful, other entities throughout creation also experience a similar change in their "motion" because we all come from the same source.

Thus, when we engage in spiritual practice, we improve our own lives, increase the love experienced by every sentient being and circulate that love throughout the world. We, in fact, become the genesis of a world that is worthy of us: the Most Beloved Children of God.

about the author

Allison V. Thompkins, Ph.D., is a spiritual practitioner who knows the transformative power of spirituality. Born with cerebral palsy, she lives a joyful life and has experienced many achievements due to her commitment to spiritual practices. These self-modified practices were designed to meet her specific needs. Inspired by the gains she made when doing these practices, Allison now develops personalized spiritual practices for clients with disabilities. Additionally, she has written articles and blog posts about spirituality, accessibility, and disability culture that have been published by outlets such as *New Mobility* magazine and *The Boston Globe.*

Since Allison holds a doctorate in economics from MIT and has served as an economics consultant to agencies around the world, you can imagine her surprise when she found herself writing a book about spirituality. However, authoring a book that combines spirituality and inclusion—two of her passions—is the culmination of years of spiritual study and the manifestation of one of her greatest dreams!

During her free time, Allison loves spending time with family and friends, traveling, watching tennis, being on the beach, creating art, and discovering new shades of purple to incorporate into her wardrobe and home decor.

For more information about Allison, visit her at **www.allisonvthompkins.com.**

endnotes

INTRODUCTION

1. CDC. 2023. "Disability Impacts All of Us Infographic." Centers for Disease Control and Prevention. May 15, 2023. https://www.cdc.gov/ncbddd/disabilityandhealth/infographic-disability-impacts-all.html.

2. Rodriguez, Valerie J., Noreen M. Glover-Graf, and E. Lisette Blanco. 2013. "Conversations with God." *Rehabilitation Counseling Bulletin* 56 (4): 215–28. https://doi.org/10.1177/0034355213477477.

3. Griffin, Megan M., Lydia W. Kane, Courtney Taylor, Susan H. Francis, and Robert M. Hodapp. 2012. "Characteristics of Inclusive Faith Communities: A Preliminary Survey of Inclusive Practices in the United States." *Journal of Applied Research in Intellectual Disabilities* 25 (4): 383–91. https://doi.org/10.1111/j.1468-3148.2011.00675.x.

4. Taylor, Courtney. n.d. "Collaborative on Faith and Disability." Collaborative on Faith & Disability. https://faithanddisability.org.

5. Jones Ault, Melinda. 2010. *Review of Participation of Families of Children with Disabilities in Their Faith Communities: A Survey of Parents*. ProQuest Central; ProQuest Dissertations & Theses Global.

6. Sumner, David E. "Preparing for Ministry to People with Disabilities." Spring 2020. Intrust.org. Accessed July 25, 2023. https://intrust.org/Magazine/Issues/Spring-2020/Preparing-for-ministry-to-people-with-disabilities.

7. "Disability Justice." n.d. http://disabilityj.blogspot.com/.

CHAPTER ONE

1. Williamson, Marianne. 2021. "Morning Meditation Day 42." TRANSFORM with Marianne Williamson. October 22, 2021. https://mariannewilliamson.substack.com/p/morning-meditation-day-42-573#details.

2. Gabriel, Roger. 2019. "5 Ways to Surrender Spiritually through Meditation." Chopra. January 4, 2019. https://chopra.com/articles/5-ways-to-surrender-spiritually-through-meditation.

3. Tolle, Eckhart. (1997) 2004. *The Power of NOW: A Guide to Spiritual Enlightenment*. Vancouver, B.C.: Namaste Pub.; Novato, CA: New World Library.

CHAPTER TWO

1. Beckwith, Reverend Michael Bernard. Agape International Spiritual Center. August 15, 2021.

2. Holmes, Ernest. 2007. *Prayer: How to Pray Effectively from the Science of Mind*. New York: TarcherPerigee.

3. Butterworth, Eric. 2017. *Practical Metaphysics: A New Insight in Truth*. New Jersey: Unity Books.

4. Unity Church of El Cajon. 2023. "Affirmative Prayer." https://www.unityofelcajon.org/affirmative-prayer.

5. Hey, Alex. 2018. "Improve Your ADHD Brain's Focus While Praying." Reset ADHD. August 6, 2018. https://www.resetadhd.com/blog/2018/7/26/improve-your-adhd-brains-focus-while-praying.

CHAPTER THREE

1. Schucman, Helen. 2019. *A Course in Miracles: Text, Workbook for Students, Manual for Teachers*. Mineola, NY: Ixia Press.

2. Richardson, Cheryl. 2005. *The Unmistakable Touch of Grace*. New York: Free Press.

3. Fillmore, Charles. 1959. The Revealing Word. Lee's Summit, MO: Unity School of Christianity.

4. Ibid.

5. Butterworth, Eric. 2010. *The Universe Is Calling: Opening to the Divine through Prayer*. New York: HarperOne.

CHAPTER FOUR

1. Richo, David. 2007. *The Power of Coincidence: How Life Shows Us What We Need to Know*. Boston: Shambhala.

2. Kerr, Laura K. 2013. "Synchronicity." In Teo, T. (ed.). *Encyclopedia of Critical Psychology*. Berlin, Heidelberg: Springer-Verlag.

3. Luna, Aletheia. 2022. "Synchronicity: 7 Ways to Interpret and Manifest It." December 6, 2022. https://lonerwolf.com/synchronicity/.

4. Shah MBE DL, Dr. Vikas, 2021. "A Conversation with Marianne Williamson – Author, Activist & Spiritual Thought Leader." Thought Economics. June 19, 2021. https://thoughteconomics.com/marianne-williamson/.

5. Beckwith, Rev. Michael Bernard. Agape International Spiritual Center. July 25, 2015.

6. Caraballo, Marlene. 2020. "Setting Intentions | A Powerful Way to Start the New Year." Cheers to Chapter Two. December 30, 2020. https://cheers2chapter2.com/setting-intentions-a-powerful-way-to-start-the-new-year.

CHAPTER FIVE

1. Amit, Ray. "101 Best Amit Ray Quotes." https://amitray.com/amitray-quotes/.

2. "Respiratory Health in Cerebral Palsy | AACPDM." n.d. American Academy for Cerebral Palsy and Developmental

Medicine. https://www.aacpdm.org/publications/care-pathways/respiratory-health-in-cerebral-palsy.

3. Schucman, Helen. 2019. *A Course in Miracles: Text, Workbook for Students, Manual for Teachers*. Mineola, NY: Ixia Press.

4. Goddard, Neville. 2013. *Feeling Is the Secret*. Jazzybee Verlag.

5. Goad, Gordon. 2019. "Top Meditation Techniques to Fight Addiction." July 12, 2019. https://www.rtor.org/2019/07/12/top-meditation-techniques-to-fight-addiction/.

CHAPTER SIX

1. Dempriey, Louix Dor. n.d. "Gratitude Is the Highest Form of Prayer." https://www.louix.org/gratitude-is-the-highest-form-of-prayer/.

2. Vanzant, Iyanla. "Iyanla Vanzant: Gratitude Is like a Magnet; the More. . . ." November 25, 2021. https://www.facebook.com/DrIyanlaVanzant/posts/gratitude-is-like-a-magnet-the-more-grateful-you-are-the-more-you-will-receive-t/5005747092791449/.

3. Ryu, Jenna, and Todd, Carolyn L. "7 Easy and Non-Corny Ways to Practice Gratitude Every Day." July 20, 2023. SELF. https://www.self.com/story/gratitude-practice-tips.

CHAPTER SEVEN

1. Williamson, Marianne. 2013. *A Year of Miracles*. New York: HarperCollins.

2. Ibid.

3. Masters, Paul Leon. 2016. "The Theocentric Way of Life," Volume 5: Module 55. International Metaphysical Ministry.

4. Hey, Alex. 2018. "Improve Your ADHD Brain's Focus While Praying." 2018. Reset ADHD. August 6, 2018. https://www.resetadhd.com/blog/2018/7/26/improve-your-adhd-brains-focus-while-praying.

CHAPTER EIGHT

1. Beckwith, Rev. Michael Bernard. Agape International Spiritual Center. May 28, 2023.

2. "Communicating with a Person in Coma." n.d. OSHO Sammasati. https://oshosammasati.org/carers/rapport-skills/coma-communication-meditation/.

3. Ibid.

FINAL WORDS

1. Williamson, Marianne. 2013. *A Year of Miracles*. New York: HarperCollins.

Hay House Titles of Related Interest

YOU CAN HEAL YOUR LIFE, the movie,
starring Louise Hay & Friends
(available as an online streaming video)
www.hayhouse.com/louise-movie

THE SHIFT, the movie,
starring Dr. Wayne W. Dyer
(available as an online streaming video)
www.hayhouse.com/the-shift-movie

***

SPIRITUAL ACTIVATOR: 5 Steps to Clearing, Unblocking, and Protecting Your Energy to Attract More Love, Joy, and Purpose, by Oliver Niño

INTIMATE CONVERSATIONS WITH THE DIVINE: Prayer, Guidance, and Grace, by Caroline Myss

THE POWER OF AWAKENING: Mindfulness Practices and Spiritual Tools to Transform Your Life, by Dr. Wayne W. Dyer

HAPPY DAYS: The Guided Path from Trauma to Profound Freedom and Inner Peace, by Gabrielle Bernstein

All of the above are available at www.hayhouse.co.uk.

CONNECT WITH HAY HOUSE ONLINE

hayhouse.co.uk
@hayhouseuk
@hayhouseuk
@hayhouse
@hayhouseuk
@hayhouseuk

Find out all about our latest books & card decks • Be the first to know about exclusive discounts • Interact with our authors in live broadcasts • Celebrate the cycle of the seasons with us • Watch free videos from your favourite authors • Connect with like-minded souls

'The gateways to wisdom and knowledge are always open.'

Louise Hay